peeking into
a box of
chocolates

REALLIFE**STUFF**FOR**WOMEN** ON TEMPTATION
A NavStudy Featuring *The* MESSAGE

Written and compiled by Karen Lee-Thorp

NAVPRESS®

BRINGING TRUTH TO LIFE

OUR GUARANTEE TO YOU

We believe so strongly in the message of our books that we are making this quality guarantee to you. If for any reason you are disappointed with the content of this book, return the title page to us with your name and address and we will refund to you the list price of the book. To help us serve you better, please briefly describe why you were disappointed. Mail your refund request to: NavPress, P.O. Box 35002, Colorado Springs, CO 80935.

The Navigators is an international Christian organization. Our mission is to reach, disciple, and equip people to know Christ and to make Him known through successive generations. We envision multitudes of diverse people in the United States and every other nation who have a passionate love for Christ, live a lifestyle of sharing Christ's love, and multiply spiritual laborers among those without Christ.

NavPress is the publishing ministry of The Navigators. NavPress publications help believers learn biblical truth and apply what they learn to their lives and ministries. Our mission is to stimulate spiritual formation among our readers.

ISBN 1-57683-835-8

Cover design by studiogearbox.com
Cover illustration by photos.com
Creative Team: Steve Parolini, Arvid Wallen, Cara Iverson, Pat Reinheimer

Written and compiled by Karen Lee-Thorp

Some of the anecdotal illustrations in this book are true to life and are included with the permission of the persons involved. All other illustrations are composites of real situations, and any resemblance to people living or dead is coincidental.

All Scripture quotations in this publication are taken from *THE MESSAGE* (MSG). Copyright © 1993, 1994, 1995, 1996, 2000, 2001, 2002. Used by permission of NavPress Publishing Group.

Printed in Canada

1 2 3 4 5 6 7 8 9 10 / 09 08 07 06 05

FOR A FREE CATALOG OF NAVPRESS BOOKS & BIBLE STUDIES,
CALL 1-800-366-7788 (USA) OR 1-800-839-4769 (CANADA)

contents

about the
REALLIFESTUFFFORWOMEN
series

Let your love dictate how you deal with me;
   teach me from your textbook on life.
I'm your servant — help me understand what that means,
   the inner meaning of your instructions. . . .
Break open your words, let the light shine out,
   let ordinary people see the meaning.

—PSALM 119:124-125,130

We're all yearning for understanding—for truth, wisdom, and hope. Whether we suffer in the simmering quiet of uncertainty or the megaphone cacophony of disbelief, we long for a better life—a more meaningful existence. We want to be Women Who Matter. But the fog of "real life stuff" we encounter every day obscures the life we crave, so we go on with the way things are.

Sometimes we pretend we don't care.

We do.

Sometimes we pretend everything is fine.

It isn't.

The truth is, the real life stuff matters. In that fog, there are things about our husbands, our children, our friends, our work, and, most significantly, ourselves that cause varying degrees of distress, discomfort, and disease.

The REAL LIFE STUFF FOR WOMEN series is a safe place for exploring the truth about that fog. But it's not a typical Bible study. You won't find any fill-in-the-blank questions in these pages. Nor will you find any pat answers. It's likely you'll come away with more questions rather than fewer. But through personal reflection and—in a small group—lively discussion (the best part of a Bible study anyway), these books will take you where you need to go and bring greater hope and meaning to your life.

Each of the books in this series provides a place to ask the hard questions of yourself and others, a place to find comfort in the chaos, a place to enlarge understanding, and—with the guidance of the Holy Spirit—a place to discover Real Life Hope that brings meaning to the everyday.

introduction

Temptation. If you're breathing, you experience it. But can a Christian woman admit to a friend that she feels tempted by any sin more serious than eating two desserts? Sure, men can talk with other men about lust. But for a woman to tell her friends, "Here's what I can't get out of my mind" or "I've done this and done this, and I know it's wrong, but I can't even make myself *want* to stop"—that puts her in a scary place. Christian women are supposed to be pure, virtuous, and innocent.

And many of us feel we are. After all, if only the big sins like adultery, pornography, theft, and abortion count, then a lot of us are off the hook. Others of us are all too aware of the desire or habit that haunts us—we just can't imagine bringing it up in a Bible study group. So we try to battle it on our own, with limited success, and every failure reinforces our shame and our commitment to hide.

This has to stop. It's time to admit that we're all tempted by something, usually a variety of things. Those things may have nothing to do with sex or chocolate, but they still matter. Sometimes we give in and sin. Sometimes we say no, and the next day we have to say no again, and again, and again. And sometimes we can see right through the temptation and thumb our noses.

We aren't meant to be the lone, proud heroines in this battle. We're supposed to be in this together. Nothing pulls the teeth from a temptation like opening up about it to a friend. But it's embarrassing. We hate being embarrassed.

Real friends will think it's fantastic that we're brave enough to name our foe.

So what tempts you? And are you tired of it enough to want it off your back?

how to
use this
discussion guide

This discussion guide is meant to be completed on your own and in a small group. So before you begin, line up a discussion group. Perhaps you already participate in a women's group. That works. Maybe you know a few friends who could do coffee once a week. That works, too. Ask around. You'll be surprised how many of your coworkers, neighbors, and children's friends' mothers would be interested in a small-group study—especially a study like this that doesn't require vast biblical knowledge. A group of four to six is optimal—any bigger and one or more members will likely be shut out of discussions. Your small group can also be two. Choose a friend who isn't afraid to "tell it like it is." Make sure each person has her own copy of the book.

1. *Read* the Scripture passages and other readings in each lesson on your own. Let it all soak in. Then use the white space provided to "think out loud on paper." Note content in the readings that troubles you, inspires you, confuses you, or challenges you. Be honest. Be bold. Don't shy away from the hard things. If you don't understand the passage, say so. If you don't agree, say that, too. You may choose to go over the material in one thirty- to forty-five-minute focused session. Or perhaps you'll spend twenty minutes a day on the readings. If the book doesn't provide enough space for you to write, use a notebook or journal.

2. *Think* about what you read. Think about what you write. Always ask, "What does this mean?" and "Why does this matter?" about the readings. Compare different Bible translations. Respond to the questions we've provided. You may have a lot to say on one topic, little on another. That's okay—this isn't a test where you have to answer every question. When you're in your small group, come back to the topics that seem most significant. Let the experience of others broaden your wisdom. You'll be stretched here—called upon to evaluate whether your conclusions make sense. In community, that stretching can often be painful and sometimes even embarrassing. But your willingness to be transparent—your openness to the possibility of personal growth—will reap great rewards.

3. *Pray* as you go through the entire session: before you read a word, in the middle of your thinking process, when you get stuck on a concept or passage, and as you approach the time when you'll explore these passages and thoughts together in a small group. Pause when you need to ask God for inspiration or when you need to cry out in frustration. Speak your prayers, be silent, or write out your prayers by using the prayer starters we've provided throughout each lesson.

4. *Live.* (That's "live" as in "rhymes with give" as in "Give me something I can really use in my life.") Before you meet with your small group, complete as much of this section as you can (particularly the "What I Want to Discuss" section). Then, in your small group, ask the hard questions about what the lesson means to you. Dig deep for relevant, reachable goals. Record your real-world plan in the book. Commit to following through on these plans, and let the other women support you in doing so. Arrange some way of checking in with each other for encouragement.

5. *Follow up.* Don't let the life application drift away without action. Let other group members ask you how your plan is going and refer to previous "Live" as in "rhymes with give" sections often. Take time at the beginning of each new study to review. See how you're doing.

6. *Repeat* as necessary.

small-group
study tips

After going through each week's study on your own, it's time to sit down with others and go deeper. Here are a few thoughts on how to make the most of your small-group discussion time.

Set ground rules. You don't need many. Here are two:

First, you'll want group members to make a commitment to the entire eight-week study. A binding legal document with notarized signatures and commitments written in blood probably isn't necessary, but you know your friends best. Just remember this: Significant personal growth happens when group members spend enough time together to really get to know each other. Hit-and-miss attendance rarely allows this to occur.

Second, agree together that everyone's story is important. Time is a valuable commodity, so if you have an hour to spend together, do your best to give each person ample time to express concerns, pass along insights, and generally feel like a participating member of the group. Small-group discussions are not monologues. However, a one-person-dominated discussion isn't always a bad thing. Your role in a small group is not only to explore and expand your own understanding; it's also to support one another. If someone truly needs more of the floor, give it to her. There will be times when the needs of the one outweigh the needs of the many. Use good judgment and allow extra space when needed. *Your* time might be next week.

Meet regularly. Choose a time and place, and stick to it. No one likes showing up to Carmine's Cafe at 12:30, only to discover the meeting was moved to Salad Celebration at noon. Consistency removes stress that could otherwise frustrate discussion and subsequent personal growth. It's only eight weeks. You can do this.

Talk openly. If you enter this study with your Happy Christian Woman mask on, you're probably not alone. And you're not a "bad person" for your hesitation to unpack your life in front of friends or strangers. Maybe you're skeptical about the value of revealing the deepest parts of who you are to others. Maybe you're simply too afraid of what might fall out of the suitcase. You don't have to go to a place where you're uncomfortable. If you want to sit and listen, offer a few thoughts, or even express a surface level of your own pain, go ahead. But don't neglect what brings you to this place—that longing for real life and real connection. You can't ignore it away. Dip your feet in the water of brutal honesty and you may choose to dive in. There is healing here.

Avoid fixing others. Sometimes it's scary when another woman takes off her Happy Christian mask. We women have an instinct to want to "make it all better" for any hurting or angry person, whether child or adult. Also, we have varying levels of tolerance for other people's negativity. Please resist your mommy instinct. Give advice only when asked, and even then, use restraint.

Stay on task. Refrain from sharing material that falls into the "too much information" category. Don't spill unnecessary stuff, such as the sexual positions your husband prefers or the in-depth details of an argument you had with your mother. This is about discovering how *you* can be a better person.

Support each other's growth. That "Live" section isn't just busywork. If you're really ready for positive change—for spiritual growth—you'll want to take this section seriously. Not only should you personally be thorough as you summarize your discoveries, practical as you compose your goals, and realistic as you determine the support you need from the group, you also need to check back with the others in the group to see if they're following through. Be lovingly honest as you examine each other's "Live" section. Don't hold back—this is where the rubber meets the road. A lack of openness here may send other group members skidding off that road.

i want what i want

the beginning place

In future lessons, we'll look at half a dozen common temptations women face, but we begin here with temptation in general. What comes to mind when you hear that word, *temptation?* Sex? Ice cream? A bad angel sitting on your shoulder? The Garden of Eden? Guilt? Fear? Frustration? Laughter? Write down what came to mind. List your:

feelings

images

beliefs and opinions

questions

If you don't want to record your darkest temptation in a book that you're not keeping under lock and key, write something in code that only you will understand. You don't have to tell your friends about your temptation if you don't want to. But at least tell yourself, sometime before the end of this study. We'll start here and then go deeper.

read it looks so good

Genesis 2:16-17; 3:1-13

In the beginning, Eve let a snake con her into eating a no-no, and we women haven't stopped taking the heat for it. You've probably heard a million references to this story, many of them misleading. See if you can take a fresh look at it.

GOD commanded the Man, "You can eat from any tree in the garden, except from the Tree-of-Knowledge-of-Good-and-Evil. Don't eat from it. The moment you eat from that tree, you're dead." . . .

The serpent was clever, more clever than any wild animal GOD had made. He spoke to the Woman: "Do I understand that God told you not to eat from any tree in the garden?"

The Woman said to the serpent, "Not at all. We can eat from the trees in the garden. It's only about the tree in the middle of the garden that God said, 'Don't eat from it; don't even touch it or you'll die.'"

The serpent told the Woman, "You won't die. God knows that the moment you eat from that tree, you'll see what's really going on. You'll be just like God, knowing everything, ranging all the way from good to evil."

When the Woman saw that the tree looked like good eating and realized what she would get out of it—she'd know everything!—she took and ate the fruit and then gave some to her husband, and he ate.

Immediately the two of them did "see what's really going on"—saw themselves naked! They sewed fig leaves together as makeshift clothes for themselves.

When they heard the sound of GOD strolling in the garden in the evening breeze, the Man and his Wife hid in the trees of the garden, hid from GOD.

GOD called to the Man: "Where are you?"

He said, "I heard you in the garden and I was afraid because I was naked. And I hid."

God said, "Who told you you were naked? Did you eat from that tree I told you not to eat from?"

The Man said, "The Woman you gave me as a companion, she gave me fruit from the tree, and, yes, I ate it."

God said to the Woman, "What is this that you've done?"

"The serpent seduced me," she said, "and I ate."

think

- What techniques did the serpent use to tempt Eve?
- Why was eating that forbidden fruit so appealing?
- Why do you think God banned the fruit?
- How did yielding to temptation change Eve?
- From this story, what can we learn about core issues that lie at the roots of all the temptations we face?
- Do any of God's commands puzzle you? If so, which ones?

pray

God, sometimes I hear the tempter saying . . .

read wise and grown-up

From *Perelandra*, by C. S. Lewis[1]

> *C. S. Lewis's novel* Perelandra *imagines the temptation of another Eve on the planet Perelandra. Here the Devil (possessing the body of a man named Weston) tempts the Lady of Perelandra to disobey Maleldil (God). Perelandra is a planet of huge oceans, many floating islands, and some fixed land masses. Maleldil has commanded the Lord and Lady of Perelandra to spend their nights on only the floating islands, not the Fixed Land.*

[The tempter said] "Have you understood that to wait for Maleldil's voice when Maleldil wishes you to walk on your own is a kind of disobedience?"

"I think I have." [said the Lady]

"The wrong kind of obeying itself can be a disobeying."

The Lady thought for a few moments and then clapped her hands. "I see," she said, "I see! Oh, how old you make me. Before now I have chased a beast for mirth. And it has understood and run away from me. If it had stood still and let me catch it, that would have been a sort of disobeying—but not the best sort."

"You understand very well. When you are fully grown you will be even wiser and more beautiful than the women of my own world. And you see that it might be so with Maleldil's biddings."

"I think I do not see quite clearly."

"Are you certain that he really wishes to be always obeyed?"

"How can we not obey what we love?"

"The beast that ran away loved you."

think

- In this story, what good desires does the tempter appeal to?
- Why is it important for the tempter to get the Lady to *imagine* what it would be like to do what Maleldil forbids?

- Most of us were tempted to do things that seemed smart and grown-up ("fully grown . . . wiser . . . more beautiful") when we were teenagers. What are the supposedly smart, grown-up things that tempt you now?

- The tempter suggests that sometimes God may not want to be obeyed. Perhaps God secretly wants us to disobey a command to show that we're growing up and learning to think for ourselves. What do you think of that argument?

- There are lots of situations (such as which house to buy) when God's Word doesn't give us a direct command about what to do. How do you think God wants us to handle situations like that?

- What insights into temptation does this story give you?

pray

Lord, to be smart and grown-up . . .

read   this throne isn't big enough for both of us

Exodus 20:2-3

> I am GOD, your God,
>> who brought you out of the land of Egypt,
>> out of a life of slavery.
> No other gods, only me.

From *Renovation of the Heart*, by Dallas Willard[2]

Human beings have always known there is a God and have had some degree of understanding of who he is and what he is like (Romans 1:19-20). Actually, they still do. But they were not pleased that he should have the place in the universe that he does have merely because he is who he is. And this is the key to understanding humanity's present condition. The first of the Ten Commandments deals with this inclination away from God (Exodus 20:2-3). As Augustine saw clearly, God being God offends human pride. If God is running the universe and has first claim on our lives, guess who *isn't* running the universe and does not get to have things as they please. . . .

Their God, as Paul elsewhere wrote, is their "belly" (Philippians 3:19, KJV), the feeling center of the self. They are willing *slaves* of their feelings or appetites (Romans 16:18). They "want what they want when they want it," as the song says, and that is the ultimate fact about them. If they do not get it they become angry and depressed, and are a danger to themselves and others.

think

- What core temptations do these two readings identify?
- When you don't get what you want, what does that teach you about God?
- Why does God have a right to be God and call the shots in the universe?

- What do you think is a reasonable Christian reaction to having your longings unfulfilled or your hopes dashed?
- Some women can't think of anything they really want. They believe biblical contentment means giving up passionate desires. What do you think about this view?

pray

You are GOD, my God, who . . .

read are we having fun yet?

James 1:2-8,12-15

Consider it a sheer gift, friends, when tests and challenges come at you from all sides. You know that under pressure, your faith-life is forced into the open and shows its true colors. So don't try to get out of anything prematurely. Let it do its work so you become mature and well-developed, not deficient in any way.

If you don't know what you're doing, pray to the Father. He loves to help. You'll get his help, and won't be condescended to when you ask for it. Ask boldly, believingly, without a second thought. People who "worry their prayers" are like wind-whipped waves. Don't think you're going to get anything from the Master that way, adrift at sea, keeping all your options open. . . .

Anyone who meets a testing challenge head-on and manages to stick it out is mighty fortunate. For such persons loyally in love with God, the reward is life and more life.

Don't let anyone under pressure to give in to evil say, "God is trying to trip me up." God is impervious to evil, and puts evil in no one's way. The temptation to give in to evil comes from us and only us. We have no one to blame but the leering, seducing flare-up of our own lust. Lust gets pregnant, and has a baby: sin! Sin grows up to adulthood, and becomes a real killer.

think

- How are hardships and challenges also temptations?
- Why does James think we should view challenges as gifts?
- How do you think a person should pray when tempted to do something wrong under pressure?
- What are some pressures that you face?
- James talks about lust. We usually think of lust as desire for sex, but the Greek word means inappropriate desire for any-thing. What are some inappropriate desires that women are especially prone to?

think (continued)

pray

Father, I admit it, I don't know what I'm doing . . .

read   you're in good (or bad) company

1 Corinthians 10:1,5-13

Remember our history, friends, and be warned. All our ancestors were led by the providential Cloud and taken miraculously through the Sea. . . . But just experiencing God's wonder and grace didn't seem to mean much—most of them were defeated by temptation during the hard times in the desert, and God was not pleased.

The same thing could happen to us. We must be on guard so that we never get caught up in wanting our own way as they did. And we must not turn our religion into a circus as they did—"First the people partied, then they threw a dance." We must not be sexually promiscuous—they paid for that, remember, with twenty-three thousand deaths in one day! We must never try to get Christ to serve us instead of us serving him; they tried it, and God launched an epidemic of poisonous snakes. We must be careful not to stir up discontent; discontent destroyed them.

These are all warning markers—DANGER!—in our history books, written down so that we don't repeat their mistakes. Our positions in the story are parallel—they at the beginning, we at the end—and we are just as capable of messing it up as they were. Don't be so naive and self-confident. You're not exempt. You could fall flat on your face as easily as anyone else. Forget about self-confidence; it's useless. Cultivate God-confidence.

No test or temptation that comes your way is beyond the course of what others have had to face. All you need to remember is that God will never let you down; he'll never let you be pushed past your limit; he'll always be there to help you come through it.

think

- Why do you suppose "experiencing God's wonder and grace" didn't keep the ancestors (Israelites in the book of Exodus) from giving in to temptation when they had to spend time in the desert?
- What do you think about the claim here that self-confidence is useless?
- What do you think Paul (the writer of this passage) would say to a woman who isn't aware of being seriously tempted to commit any sins?
- Does it comfort you to know that others have been through the same temptations you face? Why or why not?
- Do you ever feel that God is pushing you past your limit? If so, when?

pray

Lord, I need your help to resist . . .

LIVE

what i want to discuss

What have you discovered this week that you definitely want to discuss with your small group? Write that here. Then begin your small-group discussion with these thoughts.

so what?

Use the following space to summarize the truths you uncovered about temptation, how you feel about those truths, and where you need to begin in dealing with your situation. Review your "Beginning Place" if you need to remember where you began. How does God's truth affect the next step in your journey?

now what?

What is one practical thing you can do to respond to what you discovered? What concrete action can you take? Remember to think realistically—an admirable but unreachable goal is as good as no goal. Discuss your goal in your small group to further define it.

how?

How can your group—or even one other person—help you follow through with the goal you described? What support do you need? How will you measure the success of your plan? Write the details here.

i am what i own

a reminder:

Before you dive into this study, spend a little time reviewing what you wrote in the previous lesson's "Live" section. How are you doing? Check with your small-group members and review your progress toward your goals. If necessary, adjust your goals and plans, and then recommit to them.

the beginning place

It's impossible to choose the top six temptations that afflict contemporary women. The top hundred would be easier. But to help you think more deeply about temptation in general, lessons 2 through 7 will examine half a dozen common temptations. You may not connect with all six, but one or two probably have your name on them.

We begin with the temptation to accumulate stuff. Think of "stuff" broadly to include not just possessions but also services (such as getting your hair colored or using your cell phone) and experiences (such as travel and entertainment). While people often think of sex as the number-one temptation, Jesus talked about the temptation of money and possessions far more than he talked about sexual lust. So did the Old Testament prophets. Stuff is a big deal.

So what role does shopping, buying, accumulating, and consuming play in your life? If you enjoy self-quizzes, try this one: How often are the following statements true of you? Rate yourself on a scale of 0 (never) to 5 (constantly).

- I shop to lift my mood.
- I envy someone else for something she possesses.
- I feel inferior because I lack some consumer good (the right clothes, hairstyle, home decorating feature, and so on).
- I feel superior because I possess some consumer good.
- I need to spend money (on cable TV, movies, eating out, and so on) in order to be entertained or enjoy my leisure time.
- I have trouble letting go of stuff that won't fit in my home or closet; I use my garage or storage unit to handle the excess.
- I spend enormous amounts of time thinking about buying.
- I believe I would be happier if my household income was more than it is now.

read stuff as self-expression

From the *U.S. News and World Report* article "Our Consuming Interest,"
by Linda Kulman[1]

"We're opting for income over free time, and that income gets
translated into consumer goods," says Juliet Schor, author of *The
Overspent American*. And if income falls short, Americans satisfy
their wants by incurring debt, which now accounts for about 110
percent of personal disposable income. . . .

Why is our appetite for stuff so insatiable? For one thing, we
have come to think that buying is an essential expression of freedom and individualism. As the old fast-food jingles went: "Gino's
gives you freedom of choice," while Burger King lets you "have
it your way." David Brooks writes in *Bobos in Paradise: The New
Upper Class and How They Got There*, "You become the curator
of your possessions . . . the Bernard Berenson of the mantel-
piece . . . each item you display will be understood to have been
a rare 'find.'"

Consumption is a competitive business, with a constant ratch-
eting up of expectations. We no longer measure ourselves against
the Joneses next door but against the people we know only from
the media. Our friends on *Friends* lived—in spite of poor to
middling incomes—in fabulous New York apartments. *Lucky* is
a women's magazine about shopping. J Lo's left hand is weighed
down by an 8-carat diamond, which makes our own finger jew-
elry look puny. But piling on of such images gives us the sense
that we need more and we need it sooner: longing for the sensa-
tion of wealth, college students put pizza on the credit cards they
are offered the first week of freshman year.

The normal pattern is "you get more money, you spend
more money," says Cornell economist Robert Frank, the author of
Luxury Fever: Why Money Fails to Satisfy in an Era of Excess. And
yet since the mid-1970s, when almost everyone's income stopped
growing, our spending patterns have kept expanding. "It's not
as if anybody is consciously trying to keep up with Bill Gates,"

Frank says. "He's not in the set we compare ourselves too. [But] it trickles down one step at a time." And it's difficult to drop out of the contest, Frank says. Real estate values are tied to the quality of local education, so parents stretch on housing for fear that if they don't, their kids will fall behind.

think

- To what extent do you believe that "buying is an essential expression of freedom and individualism"?
- How, if at all, do you express yourself through buying?
- What aspects, if any, of your appearance and possessions do you compare to people in the media? How does that affect your feelings? Your actions?
- Are you in debt? If so, how did you get there?
- What kinds of "stuff" tempt you the most? What do you find so tempting about that stuff?

pray

Lord, my appetite for stuff . . .

read   i need a bigger garage

From the *Los Angeles Times* article "Psychology by the Square Foot,"
by Victoria Clayton[2]

About 1,400 of the estimated 31,000 self-storage facilities in the
United States are in Southern California, with each area facility
averaging 55,000 square feet.

The phenomenal popularity of EBay is fueled in part by
those obsessed with collecting everything from Disney ceramic
bells to Tiger Woods Wheaties boxes, then trying to sell it to others with the same acquisitive impulse. A recent visit to EBay's
collectibles category found 1,562,773 items offered. Given the
tendencies of the sellers, it's not hard to imagine them doing a
little compulsive shopping while they're online checking the lat-
est bids. One suspects they're the same people fueling the scrap-
book craze.

Russell Belk, a professor at the University of Utah who studies possessiveness and materialism, says that our impulse to
acquire and keep things serves a function. "Our possessions
remind us of who we are," he says.

Luke 12:15-21

Speaking to the people, [Jesus] went on, "Take care! Protect yourself against the least bit of greed. Life is not defined by what you
have, even when you have a lot."

Then he told them this story: "The farm of a certain rich man
produced a terrific crop. He talked to himself: 'What can I do?
My barn isn't big enough for this harvest.' Then he said, 'Here's
what I'll do: I'll tear down my barns and build bigger ones. Then
I'll gather in all my grain and goods, and I'll say to myself, Self,
you've done well! You've got it made and can now retire. Take it
easy and have the time of your life!'

"Just then God showed up and said, 'Fool! Tonight you die.
And your barnful of goods—who gets it?'

"That's what happens when you fill your barn with Self and not with God."

think

- Jesus says, "Life is not defined by what you have." Why do you think people often define themselves by what they have?
- What point does Jesus intend to make with his story about the rich man?
- Do you collect things? If so, what do you enjoy about that?
- How do you respond to the statement, "Our possessions remind us of who we are"?
- How full of stuff is your home? Your garage? Your storage unit? Why do you think that's the case?

pray

Jesus, my barn . . .

read   where's your treasure?

Matthew 6:24

"You can't worship two gods at once. Loving one god, you'll end up hating the other. Adoration of one feeds contempt for the other. You can't worship God and Money both."

Luke 12:25-34

"Has anyone by fussing before the mirror ever gotten taller by so much as an inch? If fussing can't even do that, why fuss at all? Walk into the fields and look at the wildflowers. They don't fuss with their appearance—but have you ever seen color and design quite like it? The ten best-dressed men and women in the country look shabby alongside them. If God gives such attention to the wildflowers, most of them never even seen, don't you think he'll attend to you, take pride in you, do his best for you?

"What I'm trying to do here is get you to relax, not be so preoccupied with *getting* so you can respond to God's *giving*. People who don't know God and the way he works fuss over these things, but you know both God and how he works. Steep yourself in God-reality, God-initiative, God-provisions. You'll find all your everyday human concerns will be met. Don't be afraid of missing out. You're my dearest friends! The Father wants to give you the very kingdom itself.

"Be generous. Give to the poor. Get yourselves a bank that can't go bankrupt, a bank in heaven far from bankrobbers, safe from embezzlers, a bank you can bank on. It's obvious, isn't it? The place where your treasure is, is the place you will most want to be, and end up being."

think

- What reasons for not being driven to acquire stuff does Jesus give in these passages?

- Why is generosity an effective way to battle the temptation to acquire stuff?
- What are the signs that a person worships money and possessions?
- Psychoanalyst Erich Fromm asked, "If I am what I have, and what I have is lost, who then am I?" To what extent do you believe you are what you own? How do your actions reflect what you really believe?

pray
Father, I worship and treasure . . .

read   a born-again consumer

From the *Christianity Today* article "Consuming Passions," by Andy Crouch[3]

This is the story of how I became a mature, fully devoted follower of the consumer economy. . . .

I think my discipleship began in earnest when I learned that there is no such thing as mere toothpaste. My mother used Colgate, but my father preferred Crest. I had to decide which kind was for me, and so began my lifelong quest to develop an ever more exquisite sense of my own tastes. (Ever since, I've been a devoted Crest user—tartar control, whitening general formula, please.) Similarly, in middle school, I learned that there is a big difference between one kind of ripped, faded, and stained jeans, which are embarrassing, and another kind, which are worth $125. It took years to develop these sensitivities, but by my first years of college, after much study, I could distinguish between a hip black T-shirt from Jhane Barnes ($110) and a cheap one from Sears ($10). At last I was beginning to grow in my consumer walk. . . .

Consuming gave me a place to belong, the makers of consumer goods assured me. I was becoming part of a worldwide family of "people like me."

Naturally, my education as a consumer didn't stop when it came to religion. Evangelical friends encouraged me to make a "personal decision for Jesus." I soon realized that Jesus had a lot to offer me—for he, too, was concerned about my needs, preferences, and tastes, and was there to help me fulfill them. I was even able to buy a Bible for people just like me—The Mobile Young Professional in a High-tech Career Study Bible. It was handy because, not having time actually to study the Bible itself, I could just consult the quick and readable notes that spoke right to my situation. How much easier could it be?

think

- The *Christianity Today* article portrays a consumer mindset. What are the core beliefs of that mindset?
- How does a consumer mindset affect a person's approach to Christian faith?
- What do you think of the statement, "Consuming gave me a place to belong"?
- What's wrong with the way of thinking that this article portrays?
- To what extent do you see your own way of thinking reflected in this article?

pray

Jesus, my tastes and preferences . . .

read you did it to me

Matthew 25:31-46

"When he finally arrives, blazing in beauty and all his angels with him, the Son of Man will take his place on his glorious throne. Then all the nations will be arranged before him and he will sort the people out, much as a shepherd sorts out sheep and goats, putting sheep to his right and goats to his left.

"Then the King will say to those on his right, 'Enter, you who are blessed by my Father! Take what's coming to you in this kingdom. It's been ready for you since the world's foundation. And here's why:

I was hungry and you fed me,
I was thirsty and you gave me a drink,
I was homeless and you gave me a room,
I was shivering and you gave me clothes,
I was sick and you stopped to visit,
I was in prison and you came to me.'

"Then those 'sheep' are going to say, 'Master, what are you talking about? When did we ever see you hungry and feed you, thirsty and give you a drink? And when did we ever see you sick or in prison and come to you?' Then the King will say, 'I'm telling the solemn truth: Whenever you did one of these things to someone overlooked or ignored, that was me—you did it to me.'

"Then he will turn to the 'goats,' the ones on his left, and say, 'Get out, worthless goats! You're good for nothing but the fires of hell. And why? Because—

I was hungry and you gave me no meal,
I was thirsty and you gave me no drink,
I was homeless and you gave me no bed,
I was shivering and you gave me no clothes,
Sick and in prison, and you never visited.'

"Then those 'goats' are going to say, 'Master, what are you talking about? When did we ever see you hungry or thirsty or homeless or shivering or sick or in prison and didn't help?'

"He will answer them, 'I'm telling the solemn truth: Whenever you failed to do one of these things to someone who was being overlooked or ignored, that was me—you failed to do it to me.'

"Then those 'goats' will be herded to their eternal doom, but the 'sheep' to their eternal reward."

think

- Why are Christians called to feed the hungry, house the homeless, and so on?
- Does this story argue against the belief that we are saved by faith, apart from works? Please explain your view.
- How does investing our resources into caring for the needy, overlooked, and ignored help us resist the temptation to worship stuff?
- What role does caring for the needy have in your life?

pray

Master, I want to be . . .

LIVE

what i want to discuss

What have you discovered this week that you definitely want to discuss with your small group? Write that here. Then begin your small-group discussion with these thoughts.

so what?

Use the following space to summarize the truths you uncovered about the temptation of "stuff," how you feel about those truths, and where you need to begin in dealing with your situation. Review your "Beginning Place" if you need to remember where you began. How does God's truth affect the next step in your journey?

now what?

What is one practical thing you can do to respond to what you discovered? What concrete action can you take? Remember to think realistically—an admirable but unreachable goal is as good as no goal. Discuss your goal in your small group to further define it.

how?

How can your group—or even one other person—help you follow through with the goal you described? What support do you need? How will you measure the success of your plan? Write the details here.

eating . . .
and not eating

a reminder:

Before you dive into this study, spend a little time reviewing what you wrote in the previous lesson's "Live" section. How are you doing? Check with your small-group members and review your progress toward your goals. If necessary, adjust your goals and plans, and then recommit to them.

the beginning place

Our society treats promiscuity as normal and eating as a sin. Television ads promote a dessert by telling us, "It's sinfully delicious!" In a cross-cultural study, "asked what comes to mind upon hearing the phrase 'chocolate cake,' Americans were more apt to say 'guilt,' while the French said 'celebration.'"[1]

There's something wrong with this picture. We called this study *Peeking into a Box of Chocolates* because that seemed like an image of temptation women could relate to. But what does that say about us as women? For one thing, we struggle to distinguish the sin of gluttony from normal eating. We also confuse dieting with the spiritual discipline of fasting. Food baffles us.

So begin this lesson by describing how you relate to food. Is eating a sinful temptation for you? What about not eating, or bingeing and purging, or the many other eating disorders that plague women? How often do you eat alone? To what degree does food occupy your thoughts in a typical day?

Try a game of word association: Beside each of the following words or phrases, write the first word or phrase that comes to mind.

food

diet

chocolate cake

sugar

fat

hunger

broccoli

feast

Before moving on, reflect on what you wrote. Think about what this tells you about your temptation with food. We'll start here and then go deeper.

read   jumbo fries and diet coke, please

Proverbs 23:19-21

> Oh listen, dear child—become wise;
>   point your life in the right direction.
> Don't drink too much wine and get drunk;
>   don't eat too much food and get fat.
> Drunks and gluttons will end up on skid row,
>   in a stupor and dressed in rags.

From the *National Geographic* article "Why Are We So Fat?" by Cathy Newman[2]

Today one out of three Americans is obese, twice as many as three decades ago, and enough for the Centers for Disease Control and Prevention to declare obesity an epidemic. . . . Adult women are now eating 335 more calories per day than they did in 1971. . . . In 2000 our reported per capita daily calorie consumption was 1,877 for women . . . roughly 300 calories more than we need. . . .

Portions have exploded since the '70s. Supersized servings of french fries and sodas are often two to five times larger than when they were introduced. Jumbo portions may appeal to our pocketbooks, but they assault our waistlines. . . .

We tend to assume that people who overeat simply lack willpower. What seems increasingly clear, however, is that the drive to overeat has strong biological underpinnings. People who are genetically susceptible to obesity don't necessarily have slow metabolisms that help their bodies hang on to fat. Instead, they may have a stronger biological drive to eat, especially in an environment where food is tasty, cheap, and plentiful. . . .

"It's like trying to treat an alcoholic in a town where there's a bar every ten feet. Bad food is cheap, heavily promoted, and engineered to taste good. Healthy food is hard to get, not promoted, and expensive." . . .

As we talk, I absently reach into a small bag of fries and scarf down the contents. [Professor Barbara] Rolls calls this "mindless eating." "We pay little attention to the actual need for food," she says. In one experiment she and her students fed subjects baked pasta. "Some days we offered a normal portion. Some days we offered a portion 50 percent bigger for the same price. If we served them 50 percent more, they ate it. They just kept eating."

think

- Why is overeating such a temptation today?
- Why do you suppose "mindless eating" is so common? Can you relate to it? What might change if you were able to actively notice when you were doing it?
- What can a person do to resist mindless eating?

pray

Father, help me understand . . .

read   jesus' weight-loss plan

Matthew 4:1-11

Next Jesus was taken into the wild by the Spirit for the Test. The
Devil was ready to give it. Jesus prepared for the Test by fasting
forty days and forty nights. That left him, of course, in a state of
extreme hunger, which the Devil took advantage of in the first
test: "Since you are God's Son, speak the word that will turn
these stones into loaves of bread."

Jesus answered by quoting Deuteronomy: "It takes more than
bread to stay alive. It takes a steady stream of words from God's
mouth."

For the second test the Devil took him to the Holy City. He
sat him on top of the Temple and said, "Since you are God's
Son, jump." The Devil goaded him by quoting Psalm 91: "He has
placed you in the care of angels. They will catch you so that you
won't so much as stub your toe on a stone."

Jesus countered with another citation from Deuteronomy:
"Don't you dare test the Lord your God."

For the third test, the Devil took him on the peak of a huge
mountain. He gestured expansively, pointing out all the earth's
kingdoms, how glorious they all were. Then he said, "They're
yours—lock, stock, and barrel. Just go down on your knees and
worship me, and they're yours."

Jesus' refusal was curt: "Beat it, Satan!" He backed his rebuke
with a third quotation from Deuteronomy: "Worship the Lord your
God, and only him. Serve him with absolute single-heartedness."

The Test was over. The Devil left. And in his place, angels!
Angels came and took care of Jesus' needs.

From *Why Beauty Matters*, by Karen Lee-Thorp and Cynthia Hicks[3]

Requesting healthful food is laudable, but when . . . our bellies
dominate our lives, we have crossed the line into gluttony.

The Bible encourages us to fast periodically in order to

remind ourselves that we live not by bread alone but by God's life-giving words. Fasting and dieting are not at all the same thing. Fasting is an act of humility and dependence upon God; dieting, except for health reasons, can be a proud act ("I can make my body look however I want it to"), whose goal is pleasing people rather than God. Dieters rarely gain more compassion for the hungry as a result of their self-deprivation, while fasters often report growing more generous. In fact, dieting can often make a person angry at being deprived, envious of those who don't need to diet, judgmental toward those who are larger than the dieter but don't watch their weight, and obsessed with food. Obsessive thinking is a common sign of an idolatrous heart. . . .

Worshiping thinness is not better than worshiping food.

think

- Why did Jesus fast?
- Consider the following: "It takes more than bread to stay alive. It takes a steady stream of words from God's mouth." How are these words relevant to you?
- The reading from *Why Beauty Matters* lists some spiritual temptations associated with dieting. Do any of those tempt you?
- What makes striving to be thin so tempting?
- Do you diet? If so, would you say that your diet has positive, negative, or no effects on your ability to love God and others?

pray

Jesus, my diet . . .

read the joy of bulimia

From *Traveling Mercies*, by Anne Lamott[4]

One week after my father was diagnosed with brain cancer, I discovered bulimia. I felt like I'd discovered the secret to life, because you could eat yourself into a state of emotional numbness but not gain weight. . . .

All right, OK: there were some problems. I was scared all the time, full of self-loathing, and my heart got funky. . . .

I would try to be good, in the puritanical sense, which meant denying my appetite. Resisting temptation meant I was good—strong, counter-animal—and I'd manage to resist fattening foods for a while. But then the jungle drums would start beating again.

I looked fine on the outside: thin, cheerful, even successful. But on the inside, I was utterly obsessed. . . . I was a spy in the world of happy eating, always hungry, or stuffed, but never full. . . .

I called a woman named Rita Groszmann. . . . I sat in her office and explained how I'd gotten started and that I wasn't ready to stop but that I was getting ready to be ready to stop. She said that was fine. I said that in fact I was going to go home that very night and eat chocolates and Mexican food and then purge. She said fine. I said, "Don't try to stop me." She said, "OK." I said, "There's nothing you can do to stop me, and it's just the way it is," and we did this for half an hour or so, until she finally said very gently that she was not going to try to take my bulimia away from me. That she in fact was never going to take anything away from me, because I would try to get it back. But she said that I have some choices.

They were ridiculous choices. . . . I'll give you a couple of examples. If I was feeling lonely and overwhelmed and about to binge, she said I could call someone up and ask them if they wanted to meet me for a movie. "Yeah," I said, "right." Or here's another good one: if I was feeling very *other*, sad and scared and overwhelmed, I could invite someone over for a meal and then see if he or she felt like going for a walk. It is only because I was raised to be Politeness Person that I did not laugh at her. It was like someone detoxing off heroin, who's itching to shoot up, being told to take up macramé.

think

- What's the appeal of bulimia?
- Why would a person eat when she feels sad or scared?
- Why do you think trying "to be good" didn't help Lamott stop bingeing and purging?
- What do you think of the choices Rita Groszmann gave Lamott?
- What do you do when you feel lonely, overwhelmed, sad, or scared? Do any harmful comforts (such as overeating) tempt you?

pray

Lord, trying to be good . . .

read   but it's *my* body, isn't it?

1 Corinthians 6:13

You know the old saying, "First you eat to live, and then you live to eat"? Well, it may be true that the body is only a temporary thing, but that's no excuse for stuffing your body with food, or indulging it with sex. Since the Master honors you with a body, honor him with your body!

Philippians 3:19-21

But easy street is a dead-end street. Those who live there make their bellies their gods; belches are their praise; all they can think of is their appetites.

But there's far more to life for us. We're citizens of high heaven! We're waiting the arrival of the Savior, the Master, Jesus Christ, who will transform our earthy bodies into glorious bodies like his own. He'll make us beautiful and whole with the same powerful skill by which he is putting everything as it should be, under and around him.

think

- What do you think it means to honor God with your body when it comes to food? How easy or difficult is that for you to do?
- How can a dieter or overeater know when she's making her belly her god?
- What can a person do if she finds that all she can think of is her appetite?
- How does your hope of future transformation affect the way you view your body now?

think (continued)

pray

God, because you made my body and you're going to transform it . . .

read   a real meal

John 6:27,35,48-58

"Don't waste your energy striving for perishable food like that. Work for the food that sticks with you, food that nourishes your lasting life, food the Son of Man provides. He and what he does are guaranteed by God the Father to last." . . .

Jesus said, "I am the Bread of Life. The person who aligns with me hungers no more and thirsts no more, ever. . . .

"I am the Bread of Life. Your ancestors ate the manna bread in the desert and died. But now here is Bread that truly comes down out of heaven. Anyone eating this Bread will not die, ever. I am the Bread—living Bread!—who came down out of heaven. Anyone who eats this Bread will live—and forever! The Bread that I present to the world so that it can eat and live is myself, this flesh-and-blood self."

At this, the Jews started fighting among themselves: "How can this man serve up his flesh for a meal?"

But Jesus didn't give an inch. "Only insofar as you eat and drink flesh and blood, the flesh and blood of the Son of Man, do you have life within you. The one who brings a hearty appetite to this eating and drinking has eternal life and will be fit and ready for the Final Day. My flesh is real food and my blood is real drink. By eating my flesh and drinking my blood you enter into me and I into you. In the same way that the fully alive Father sent me here and I live because of him, so the one who makes a meal of me lives because of me. This is the Bread from heaven. Your ancestors ate bread and later died. Whoever eats this Bread will live always."

think

- How does a person eat and drink the flesh and blood of the Son of Man?
- Why do you think Jesus chose such a graphic way of talking about this?

- How can you get more nourishment from the Bread of Life?
- Do you see any connection between a woman's struggles with food and what Jesus offers in this passage? If so, what do you see?

pray

Jesus, eating your flesh and drinking your blood . . .

LIVE

what i want to discuss

What have you discovered this week that you definitely want to discuss with your small group? Write that here. Then begin your small-group discussion with these thoughts.

so what?

Use the following space to summarize the truths you uncovered about the temptation of food, how you feel about those truths, and where you need to begin in dealing with your situation. Review your "Beginning Place" if you need to remember where you began. How does God's truth affect the next step in your journey?

now what?

What is one practical thing you can do to respond to what you discovered? What concrete action can you take? Remember to think realistically—an admirable but unreachable goal is as good as no goal. Discuss your goal in your small group to further define it.

how?

How can your group—or even one other person—help you follow through with the goal you described? What support do you need? How will you measure the success of your plan? Write the details here.

giving up

a reminder:

Before you dive into this study, spend a little time reviewing what you wrote in the previous lesson's "Live" section. How are you doing? Check with your small-group members and review your progress toward your goals. If necessary, adjust your goals and plans, and then recommit to them.

the beginning place

Some of us aren't the least bit obsessed with stuff or with food. We wouldn't dream of committing a "big" sin like murder, adultery, or theft. We don't struggle with inappropriate desires. In fact, we desire very little. We call our lack of desire "contentment." Too often, though, what we call *contentment* is really *giving up*.

Passionately wanting things has gotten us nowhere—at best disappointment, and at worst big mistakes. So we've given up wanting. We don't ask God for much. We don't try to accomplish anything significant. We stay busy with things that ultimately don't matter. Or we lower our standards and just try to get by.

Some of us have good reasons for giving up. We've tried and tried at something that was really important, but we feel we've failed. We're exhausted. The line on our gas gauge is way below the red zone. We don't even claim we have contentment. We know we're not happy, but we don't know what to do about it other than lie down and die.

What comes to mind when you think of the phrase "giving up"?

A sigh of relief, a moan of despair, the furrowed brow of puzzlement? Maybe you have the kind of personality that can't imagine giving up. If so, your job in this lesson will be to learn to understand those who can. Maybe you've been thinking about giving up, or maybe you gave up a long time ago. Whatever your starting place is, take a few minutes to describe it.

read   dying by inches

From *Grace at Bender Springs*, by Vinita Hampton Wright[1]

The song came to an end, Mrs. Becket brought the piece to a tasteful close, and the congregation murmured their amens. Sarah took her seat beside Miranda, and Mom leaned over, her eyes wide with concern. "Are you feeling sick?" Sarah nodded, then left her seat and headed for the bathroom in the back. She didn't even look to see if Jacob had noticed or if anyone else could tell that something awful had happened.

She got to the bathroom but discovered that that wasn't far enough, so she slipped out the church's back door and stepped carefully through the scratchy summer grass to the small storage building. Of course it was locked. But on the west side of it a large wooden crate was overturned in the shade of a small maple tree. Beyond that were an alley and warehouses, and no one was around. Sarah sat on the crate while her heart pounded.

"I can't do this anymore, God," she said finally, after nearly five minutes had passed. She didn't close her eyes or look toward heaven. If God was around, he either wanted to hear what she had to say, or he didn't. But she had to say it. It was all exploding inside her, about to wipe out everything in its path.

"I can't do this anymore. I'm hurting these people just by being here. I don't add a single thing to their existence. I don't fit here; I don't have gifts anybody cares about. I don't think my husband loves me much anymore. My children need a better mother, and I can't be a better anything here."

The pain went too deep for tears. Sarah continued to talk at the maple tree, the summer air. "Jacob doesn't deserve this, but I've got to tell him that I need to leave now. I'm dying by inches, but nobody sees. I didn't see until just now. This minute it's finally clear to me. I can't do this. I can't do this."

think

- What do you think Sarah is being tempted to do?
- Do you see anything good in what's happening with Sarah? If so, what? If not, why not?
- If Sarah confided her feelings to you, what would you say and do?
- Have you ever felt like Sarah? If so, what was (or is) that like for you?

pray

God, that phrase, "I can't do this" . . .

read they really are out to get me

1 Kings 19:1-18

Ahab reported to Jezebel everything that Elijah had done, including the massacre of the prophets. Jezebel immediately sent a messenger to Elijah with her threat: "The gods will get you for this and I'll get even with you! By this time tomorrow you'll be as dead as any one of those prophets."

When Elijah saw how things were, he ran for dear life to Beersheba, far in the south of Judah. He left his young servant there and then went on into the desert another day's journey. He came to a lone broom bush and collapsed in its shade, wanting in the worst way to be done with it all—to just die: "Enough of this, GOD! Take my life—I'm ready to join my ancestors in the grave!" Exhausted, he fell asleep under the lone broom bush.

Suddenly an angel shook him awake and said, "Get up and eat!"

He looked around and, to his surprise, right by his head were a loaf of bread baked on some coals and a jug of water. He ate the meal and went back to sleep.

The angel of GOD came back, shook him awake again, and said, "Get up and eat some more—you've got a long journey ahead of you."

He got up, ate and drank his fill, and set out. Nourished by that meal, he walked forty days and nights, all the way to the mountain of God, to Horeb. When he got there, he crawled into a cave and went to sleep.

Then the word of GOD came to him: "So Elijah, what are you doing here?"

"I've been working my heart out for the GOD-of-the-Angel-Armies," said Elijah. "The people of Israel have abandoned your covenant, destroyed the places of worship, and murdered your prophets. I'm the only one left, and now they're trying to kill me."

Then he was told, "Go, stand on the mountain at attention before GOD. GOD will pass by."

A hurricane wind ripped through the mountains and shattered

the rocks before GOD, but GOD wasn't to be found in the wind; after the wind an earthquake, but GOD wasn't in the earthquake; and after the earthquake fire, but GOD wasn't in the fire; and after the fire a gentle and quiet whisper.

When Elijah heard the quiet voice, he muffled his face with his great cloak, went to the mouth of the cave, and stood there. A quiet voice asked, "So Elijah, now tell me, what are you doing here?" Elijah said it again, "I've been working my heart out for GOD, the GOD-of-the-Angel-Armies, because the people of Israel have abandoned your covenant, destroyed your places of worship, and murdered your prophets. I'm the only one left, and now they're trying to kill me."

GOD said, "Go back the way you came through the desert to Damascus. When you get there anoint Hazael; make him king over Aram. Then anoint Jehu son of Nimshi; make him king over Israel. Finally, anoint Elisha son of Shaphat from Abel Meholah to succeed you as prophet. Anyone who escapes death by Hazael will be killed by Jehu; and anyone who escapes death by Jehu will be killed by Elisha. Meanwhile, I'm preserving for myself seven thousand souls: the knees that haven't bowed to the god Baal, the mouths that haven't kissed his image."

think

- What emotions does Elijah feel in this passage?
- How is the way Elijah talks to God like or unlike the way you talk to God?
- What impression do you get of God in this passage?
- How does God help Elijah overcome the temptation to give up?
- What does Elijah have to do to benefit from God's help?

think (continued)

pray

God, if you asked me, "What are you doing here?" I would say . . .

read i've got everything under control

From *The Sacred Romance*, by Brent Curtis and John Eldredge[2]

Resignation is not just the sigh that groans with something gone wrong. . . . Resignation is the acceptance of the loss as final. . . . It is the condition in which we choose to see good as no longer startling in its beauty and boldness, but simply as "nice." Evil is no longer surprising; it is normal. It is from this place of heart resignation where many of us, perhaps all of us at one time or another, having suffered under the storm of life's Arrows, given up on the Sacred Romance. But our hearts will not totally forsake the intimacy and adventure we were made for and so we compromise. We both become, and take to ourselves, lovers that are less dangerous [than God] in their passion for life and the possible pain that comes with it—in short, lovers that are less wild. . . .

[W]e tend to fall into two groups when it comes to taking up housekeeping with these less-wild lovers—lovers who promise to deliver us from the Haunting of the Sacred Romance God has placed in our heart. Those of us in the first group choose anesthesia of the heart through some form of *competence* or *order*. These may be expressed in countless arenas: a clean desk, perfect housekeeping, Scripture memory and Bible study, a manicured lawn, a spotless garage, preparing and hostessing dinner parties that would make Martha Stewart proud, sending your boys to the best sports camps to ensure they (we) never experience disappointment that might provoke thirst, formulaic religion that has three-step solutions to every problem—the list is endless.

think

- What past or current experiences tempt you to see evil as normal?
- What do you think of the idea that God is "dangerous" in his "passion for life and the possible pain that comes with it"?

- How important are competence and order to you? How does your life reflect that?
- Do you think your life indicates that you've given up on bold goodness and a passionate God? What makes you say that?

pray

God, passion to me is . . .

read   it's too hard

From the *Books and Culture* article "The Enigma of Anger," by Garret Keizer[3]

> I have . . . grown increasingly angry at our full-bellied acquies-
> cence to social and economic injustice. I'm referring to the notion
> that everything other than the perfectible self is too vast and com-
> plex to admit to any remedy whatsoever, and that our best course
> of (in)action lies in ironical detachment or in the cultivation of an
> abrasive attitude that delivers some of the release, but packs none
> of the punch, of well-aimed rage. Our advertising and even our
> arts convey the idea that we as a society are brash, irreverent, and
> free of all constraints, when the best available evidence would sug-
> gest that we are in fact tame, spayed, and easily brought to heel.

Isaiah 58:6-12

> "This is the kind of fast day I'm after:
>> to break the chains of injustice,
>> get rid of exploitation in the workplace,
>> free the oppressed,
>> cancel debts.
> What I'm interested in seeing you do is:
>> sharing your food with the hungry,
>> inviting the homeless poor into your homes,
>> putting clothes on the shivering ill-clad,
>> being available to your own families.
> Do this and the lights will turn on,
>> and your lives will turn around at once.
> Your righteousness will pave your way.
>> The GOD of glory will secure your passage.
> Then when you pray, GOD will answer.
>> You'll call out for help and I'll say, 'Here I am.'
>
> "If you get rid of unfair practices,
>> quit blaming victims,

quit gossiping about other people's sins,
If you are generous with the hungry
    and start giving yourselves to the down-and-out,
Your lives will begin to glow in the darkness,
    your shadowed lives will be bathed in sunlight.
I will always show you where to go.
    I'll give you a full life in the emptiest of places—
    firm muscles, strong bones.
You'll be like a well-watered garden,
    a gurgling spring that never runs dry.
You'll use the old rubble of past lives to build anew,
    rebuild the foundations from out of your past.
You'll be known as those who can fix anything,
    restore old ruins, rebuild and renovate,
    make the community livable again."

think

- Why do you think some Christians give up on addressing social and economic injustice?
- Are you "tame, spayed, and easily brought to heel"? What makes you say that?
- When you contemplate doing the things God names in Isaiah 58, what feelings and thoughts go through your mind?
- To which of the things God names do you devote time and energy?

pray

God, please help me . . .

read   eyes on the prize

Hebrews 12:1-13

Do you see what this means—all these pioneers who blazed
the way, all these veterans cheering us on? It means we'd better get on with it. Strip down, start running—and never quit! No
extra spiritual fat, no parasitic sins. Keep your eyes on *Jesus*, who
both began and finished this race we're in. Study how he did
it. Because he never lost sight of where he was headed—that
exhilarating finish in and with God—he could put up with
anything along the way: cross, shame, whatever. And now he's
there, in the place of honor, right alongside God. When you find
yourselves flagging in your faith, go over that story again, item
by item, that long litany of hostility he plowed through. *That* will
shoot adrenaline into your souls!

In this all-out match against sin, others have suffered far
worse than you, to say nothing of what Jesus went through—all
that bloodshed! So don't feel sorry for yourselves. Or have you
forgotten how good parents treat children, and that God regards
you as *his* children?

> My dear child, don't shrug off God's discipline,
>   but don't be crushed by it either.
> It's the child he loves that he disciplines;
>   the child he embraces, he also corrects.

God is educating you; that's why you must never drop out.
He's treating you as dear children. This trouble you're in isn't
punishment; it's training, the normal experience of children.
Only irresponsible parents leave children to fend for themselves.
Would you prefer an irresponsible God? We respect our own parents for training and not spoiling us, so why not embrace God's
training so we can truly *live?* While we were children, our parents
did what *seemed* best to them. But God is doing what *is* best for
us, training us to live God's holy best. At the time, discipline isn't

much fun. It always feels like it's going against the grain. Later, of course, it pays off handsomely, for it's the well-trained who find themselves mature in their relationship with God.

So don't sit around on your hands! No more dragging your feet! Clear the path for long-distance runners so no one will trip and fall, so no one will step in a hole and sprain an ankle. Help each other out. And run for it!

think

- What, if anything, in this passage encourages you to keep going?
- If a woman found this passage overwhelming rather than motivating, what would you say to her?
- This passage says, "Don't feel sorry for yourselves." Does that mean we should never admit that we feel like giving up? Please explain your view.
- Sometimes it's extremely hard to imagine that something bad we're going through is training. It's hard to imagine that God our Parent would allow something we would never put our children through. How do you think we should come to terms with this?

pray

Father, I want to keep going . . .

LIVE

what i want to discuss

What have you discovered this week that you definitely want to discuss with your small group? Write that here. Then begin your small-group discussion with these thoughts.

so what?

Use the following space to summarize the truths you uncovered about the temptation to give up, how you feel about those truths, and where you need to begin in dealing with your situation. Review your "Beginning Place" if you need to remember where you began. How does God's truth affect the next step in your journey?

now what?

What is one practical thing you can do to respond to what you discovered? What concrete action can you take? Remember to think realistically—an admirable but unreachable goal is as good as no goal. Discuss your goal in your small group to further define it.

how?

How can your group—or even one other person—help you follow through with the goal you described? What support do you need? How will you measure the success of your plan? Write the details here.

more than
"just friends"

a reminder:

Before you dive into this study, spend a little time reviewing what you wrote in the previous lesson's "Live" section. How are you doing? Check with your small-group members and review your progress toward your goals. If necessary, adjust your goals and plans, and then recommit to them.

the beginning place

Romance novels account for more than one-third of all fiction sales in the United States, according to studies by the Romance Writers of America. That added up to $1.52 billion in 2001. Nearly every one of those dollars is spent by women.

Why the big bucks? Some say romance novels and soap operas are to women what porn is to men: fantasies that feed a hunger for intimacy and pleasure that the person isn't getting from actual relationships. The porn analogy doesn't apply to every romantic book and film, yet these works are certainly tapping into *something* inside a lot of women.

And some of us aren't just staying home with a good book. Premarital sex, adultery, emotional entanglements with married men that stop just short of physical consummation—a lot of us are looking for love in questionable places. God made us to need intimacy the way we need air, and when our world doesn't provide as much of it as we long for, we're sorely tempted to take matters into our own hands.

If you're happily married and/or have learned to receive the intimacy you need from God and your girlfriends, you may not feel temptation in this area. But chances are that somebody in your small group is struggling and needs a safe place to talk about it.

Where are you right now regarding sexual temptation? Do you have a fantasy life that has nothing to do with your husband? Do you have a male friend who understands you better than your husband can? Are you a single woman tired of waiting for marital bliss? Have you yielded to temptation in the past and now struggle with the aftereffects? Has sexual abuse left a hole in your heart? Wherever your starting place is, try to put it into words.

read   what women want

Song of Songs 4:6-15

> The sweet, fragrant curves of your body,
>> the soft, spiced contours of your flesh
> Invite me, and I come. I stay
>> until dawn breathes its light and night slips away.
> You're beautiful from head to toe, my dear love,
>> beautiful beyond compare, absolutely flawless.
>
> Come with me from Lebanon, my bride.
>> Leave Lebanon behind, and come.
> Leave your high mountain hideaway.
>> Abandon your wilderness seclusion,
> Where you keep company with lions
>> and panthers guard your safety.
> You've captured my heart, dear friend.
>> You looked at me, and I fell in love.
>> One look my way and I was hopelessly in love!
> How beautiful your love, dear, dear friend—
>> far more pleasing than a fine, rare wine,
>> your fragrance more exotic than select spices.
> The kisses of your lips are honey, my love,
>> every syllable you speak a delicacy to savor.
> Your clothes smell like the wild outdoors,
>> the ozone scent of high mountains.
> Dear lover and friend, you're a secret garden,
>> a private and pure fountain.
> Body and soul, you are paradise,
>> a whole orchard of succulent fruits—
> Ripe apricots and peaches,
>> oranges and pears;
> Nut trees and cinnamon,
>> and all scented woods;

Mint and lavender,
    and all herbs aromatic;
A garden fountain, sparkling and splashing,
    fed by spring waters from the Lebanon mountains.

think

- The Song of Songs was composed for a wedding, and 4:6-15 is how the Bible portrays the ideal of marital sex. What do you feel when you read the passage?
- The Song of Songs is often interpreted as symbolizing the love between God and his people. Imagine God saying the things in this passage. How do you respond?
- Has any man ever made you feel this desirable? If so, who and how? If not, how do you feel about that?
- What do you want from a man sexually? Emotionally?

pray

God, I want . . .

read   my husband doesn't understand me

From *NOT "Just Friends,"* by Shirley P. Glass and Jean Coppock Staeheli[1]

When Ralph first started working with Lara, they didn't talk about their marriages, except in general, positive terms. . . . For quite a while, Ralph and Lara delighted to be such compatible coworkers. They helped each other out; they laughed; they shared the same basic philosophy of life. They bonded over the television show *The Sopranos*. Every Monday morning they would avidly debrief on the previous night's episode. Talking about the characters and their predicaments gave them a way to get to know each other. Ralph couldn't help contrasting Lara's enthusiasm with his wife's hatred of the program. . . .

Things began to heat up when Ralph began to fudge on the marriage-saving precautions he and [his wife] Rachel had always followed. Over time, he began to share more of himself with Lara than with his wife. Part of the reason was simply that Rachel and Ralph had less time together than they used to. When they met, Rachel was a nurse in a pediatric intensive care unit. After they married and had children, they decided it would be best for their family if Rachel worked on the weekend, when Ralph was home. . . . This arrangement kept Ralph and Rachel so busy with the children that they didn't have much couple time. . . . Ralph found himself hungry for the stimulating conversations he could have with Lara.

Ralph and Lara went from being glad to see each other, to wishing they didn't have to deal with other people, to sneaking time alone. And when they were alone, they began to reveal more and more of themselves. Ralph would say, "I've never told anyone this before." Lara would sometimes cry when she told Ralph about her unhappy marriage and painful childhood memories. When they talked about their desires and aspirations, it felt as if they had never been so close to the heart of their own lives. They allowed their liking for each other to become a major fascination. The problem wasn't that they were attracted but that they began to act on their feelings as if they had no other primary commitments. . . .

Emotional affairs are characterized by *secrecy, emotional intimacy,* and *sexual chemistry.* These three elements can combine into a potent brew that intensifies the attraction that already exists. If the relationship is an open book, it is probably a friendship. When attempts are made to hide feelings or interactions, the friendship is becoming something else. When there is more companionship, intellectual sharing, and understanding in the friendship than in the marriage, that's also a warning signal. Sexual chemistry, an undercurrent of arousal and desire, is only enflamed by admissions that a sexual attraction exists but won't be acted on.

think

- Why is Ralph vulnerable to temptation here? What about Lara?
- Do you think Lara longs for what the Song of Songs describes? What makes you say that?
- Do you think it would make a difference if Ralph and his wife made it a priority to spend more time together without the kids? Why or why not?
- Are there things you can confide to a male friend that you can't talk to your husband about? If so, why do you think that's the case?
- Sometimes single women find themselves in Lara's position, and they often get the blame if the man's marriage breaks up. What responsibility does the single woman bear in that situation? What about the man? The man's wife?

pray

Lord, in my friendships with men . . .

read   i hate sex

From *Sex and the Soul of a Woman*, by Paula Rinehart[2]

Claire is a lovely woman about thirty years old, married to a man she met . . . in the law firm where she works. She is not too happy about being in a counselor's office, but she has to talk to somebody. . . .

"Well," she starts in slowly, "it's sex. The problem is that I hate sex." . . .

I hear this statement often these days.

Claire goes on to describe why she finds this part of her life so disagreeable. It's boring, she's been there before, she feels a trifle used—though she's not sure where this feeling comes from. She and her husband became Christians a few years ago, and she hoped this would change her feelings about sex, but it hasn't. "I could live my whole life and never miss sex." She almost whispers the words. She feels so guilty. After all, she's only thirty. Her husband is tired, not of sex but of her disinterest. He hints that he can't live like this—not feeling wanted sexually by his wife. Claire is beginning to panic.

Somewhere in this conversation, Claire starts to turn the pages of her life back ten years. She begins to talk about the first time she had sex.

"I didn't want to have a bad experience in losing my virginity—like some of my friends," she says. "So I found a guy I didn't feel anything special for, and I had sex with him. That way I could just get it over with."

"Losing your virginity was something you wanted to 'just get over'?" I think I must have heard Claire wrong.

"Well, sure. That way I wouldn't get hurt, or so I thought. Then maybe I would enjoy sex with guys I really cared about."

Somehow things didn't go according to plan. Sex became something Claire did to keep a relationship with a guy. Over the years, there were a lot of guys, including the man she eventually married. She loves him, but sex is stuck in the place it began for her. She knows it should be different, now that she is married.

"On my honeymoon, I could feel the jail bars coming down," Claire confesses. She saw herself facing a lifetime of feeling reluctant and used. She just hadn't expected that it would affect the overall health of her marriage this much.

think

- Why would a girl be tempted to get the loss of her virginity over with?
- Why would a woman be tempted to have sex just to keep a relationship with a guy?
- What temptations does Claire face now?
- How is your story like or unlike Claire's?
- If Claire had a small group like yours, what do you think she would need from you?

pray

God, my past experiences . . .

read   more than skin on skin

1 Corinthians 6:12-20

Just because something is technically legal doesn't mean that it's spiritually appropriate. If I went around doing whatever I thought I could get by with, I'd be a slave to my whims.

You know the old saying, "First you eat to live, and then you live to eat"? Well, it may be true that the body is only a temporary thing, but that's no excuse for stuffing your body with food, or indulging it with sex. Since the Master honors you with a body, honor him with your body!

God honored the Master's body by raising it from the grave. He'll treat yours with the same resurrection power. Until that time, remember that your bodies are created with the same dignity as the Master's body. You wouldn't take the Master's body off to a whorehouse, would you? I should hope not.

There's more to sex than mere skin on skin. Sex is as much spiritual mystery as physical fact. As written in Scripture, "The two become one." Since we want to become spiritually one with the Master, we must not pursue the kind of sex that avoids commitment and intimacy, leaving us more lonely than ever—the kind of sex that can never "become one." There is a sense in which sexual sins are different from all others. In sexual sin we violate the sacredness of our own bodies, these bodies that were made for God-given and God-modeled love, for "becoming one" with another. Or didn't you realize that your body is a sacred place, the place of the Holy Spirit? Don't you see that you can't live however you please, squandering what God paid such a high price for? The physical part of you is not some piece of property belonging to the spiritual part of you. God owns the whole works. So let people see God in and through your body.

think

- According to this passage, why is sex without commitment and true intimacy such a mistake?
- Have you had any experiences that make it hard for you to think of your body as a sacred place? If so, talk about what happened and how it has affected you.
- How does this passage apply to Claire in the reading from *Sex and the Soul of a Woman* (see previous "Read" section)?
- What relevance, if any, does this passage have to women who have emotional entanglements or fantasize about having affairs?

pray

Lord Jesus, my body . . .

read sex and the single girl

From the *Christianity Today* article "Solitary Refinement," by Lauren F. Winner[3]

While all Christians are called to chastity, for married folks that means forsaking all others besides their spouse. For the rest of us, it means forsaking sex, period. This is tough enough when you're 19 and single. It's an even greater challenge if you're still single—or single again—at 32.

As more Christians are single longer and longer, we need to think about sex. The issue is not whether we want to cave into cultural pressures and toss the church's teachings about sexual morality out the window; instead it's why many single Christians do not give those teachings the time of day, and what we can do to help people live chastely after, say, college. "It's difficult sexually to keep on keeping on as one year stretches into five," says Julia Duin, 44, assistant national editor of *The Washington Times* and author of *Purity Makes the Heart Grow Stronger* (Servant).

Debra Farrington agrees. "Sex is a complicated question, and we just don't speak about it. There should be an opportunity for conversation in the church, but the church is too busy seeing no evil and hearing no evil, so singles hang out alone."

What we need, it seems, are at least three things. First, we need venues for frank communication. A single Christian ought to be able to sit down with her pastor and say, "My boyfriend and I are finding it harder to only go as far as kissing, and I'm not sure what to do about that," without fearing that he'll never again take her seriously as a committed Christian.

Second, we should not act like sex outside of marriage is the unforgivable sin. A sin, indeed, but one of many that Christians struggle with. It is likely that more Christians ignore the biblical prohibition against gossip than are engaging in premarital sex, but the church is more exercised about the latter issue than the former. When we place too much emphasis on one sin, we risk not only hypocrisy, but we also make it harder for those guilty of that sin to come openly to the church for help.

Finally, we need to do more than just point to a couple of verses in Paul's epistles that warn against fornication; we need to present single Christians with a whole theology of chastity and sexuality.

think

- Whether you're married or single, describe your reaction to this reading. Did you find anything surprising? Anything you agree or disagree with?
- Do you believe sex outside marriage is worse than most other sins a woman might commit? Why or why not?
- If a single friend came to you and said she and her boyfriend were having trouble going no further than kissing, what would you say to her?
- For the married women: If you were suddenly widowed, how hard would it be for you to abstain from sex for five or ten years? Why is that?

pray

Lord, a single woman . . .

read   restoration

Luke 7:36-50

One of the Pharisees asked him over for a meal. He went to the
Pharisee's house and sat down at the dinner table. Just then a
woman of the village, the town harlot, having learned that Jesus
was a guest in the home of the Pharisee, came with a bottle of
very expensive perfume and stood at his feet, weeping, raining
tears on his feet. Letting down her hair, she dried his feet, kissed
them, and anointed them with the perfume. When the Pharisee
who had invited him saw this, he said to himself, "If this man
was the prophet I thought he was, he would have known what
kind of woman this is who is falling all over him."

Jesus said to him, "Simon, I have something to tell you."

"Oh? Tell me."

"Two men were in debt to a banker. One owed five hundred
silver pieces, the other fifty. Neither of them could pay up, and
so the banker canceled both debts. Which of the two would be
more grateful?"

Simon answered, "I suppose the one who was forgiven the
most."

"That's right," said Jesus. Then turning to the woman, but
speaking to Simon, he said, "Do you see this woman? I came to
your home; you provided no water for my feet, but she rained
tears on my feet and dried them with her hair. You gave me
no greeting, but from the time I arrived she hasn't quit kissing
my feet. You provided nothing for freshening up, but she has
soothed my feet with perfume. Impressive, isn't it? She was forgiven many, many sins, and so she is very, very grateful. If the
forgiveness is minimal, the gratitude is minimal."

Then he spoke to her: "I forgive your sins."

That set the dinner guests talking behind his back: "Who
does he think he is, forgiving sins!"

He ignored them and said to the woman, "Your faith has
saved you. Go in peace."

think

- What does this story have to say to women who have yielded to sexual temptation in the past?
- What does it say to women who haven't?
- Is there anything in this story that would help a woman resist temptation, sexual or otherwise? If so, what?
- How grateful are you to Jesus? What do your actions say?

pray

Jesus, thank you so much for . . .

LIVE

what i want to discuss

What have you discovered this week that you definitely want to discuss with your small group? Write that here. Then begin your small-group discussion with these thoughts.

so what?

Use the following space to summarize the truths you uncovered about sexual temptation, how you feel about those truths, and where you need to begin in dealing with your situation. Review your "Beginning Place" if you need to remember where you began. How does God's truth affect the next step in your journey?

now what?

What is one practical thing you can do to respond to what you discovered? What concrete action can you take? Remember to think realistically—an admirable but unreachable goal is as good as no goal. Discuss your goal in your small group to further define it.

how?

How can your group—or even one other person—help you follow through with the goal you described? What support do you need? How will you measure the success of your plan? Write the details here.

what people think

a reminder:

Before you dive into this study, spend a little time reviewing what you wrote in the previous lesson's "Live" section. How are you doing? Check with your small-group members and review your progress toward your goals. If necessary, adjust your goals and plans, and then recommit to them.

the beginning place

Alison is a low-level supervisor at a high-tech corporation. Over lunch, her colleague Sharon blows off steam about the insane deadlines and take-no-prisoners corporate politics at their company. She comments that Alison never seems to get anxious or bitter, even after she was recently stabbed in the back by a colleague competing with Alison for a promotion. Sharon asks Alison for her secret. Alison wants to say it's her faith, but Sharon has a low opinion of religion, and Alison doesn't want to get known around the company as "one of those Christians."

Also, Sharon is going through a divorce and talks about her loneliness. Alison has thought about inviting her to a gathering of single Christian friends, but Sharon dresses provocatively and laces her conversation with the "f" word. Alison worries about what her Christian friends would think.

Many of us live in bondage to what other people think. As with Alison, this fear can make us duck opportunities to share our faith. The craving for approval fuels other temptations as well, such as covetousness (the temptation to buy stuff to impress or keep up with others) and envy (resentment of those who have things we desire but don't have). We can even join others in a sin, such as gossip or snubbing "outsiders," in order to be accepted by the group.

Take a moment to write what comes to mind (feelings, images, responses) when you think of the question, "What will people think?" We'll start here and then go deeper.

read an embarrassing husband!

2 Samuel 6:12-23

"The Chest of God" (also called the ark of the covenant) was the holiest treasure in Israel. God's powerful presence accompanied it. Michal was David's wife, the daughter of the previous king. The "priest's linen" David wore did not include underwear, so if a man danced too wildly in it . . . well, you get the point.

It was reported to King David that GOD had prospered Obed-Edom and his entire household because of the Chest of God. So David thought, "I'll get that blessing for myself," and went and brought up the Chest of God from the house of Obed-Edom to the City of David, celebrating extravagantly all the way, with frequent sacrifices of choice bulls. David, ceremonially dressed in priest's linen, danced with great abandon before GOD. The whole country was with him as he accompanied the Chest of GOD with shouts and trumpet blasts. But as the Chest of GOD came into the City of David, Michal, Saul's daughter, happened to be looking out a window. When she saw King David leaping and dancing before GOD, her heart filled with scorn.

They brought the Chest of GOD and set it in the middle of the tent pavilion that David had pitched for it. Then and there David worshiped, offering burnt offerings and peace offerings. When David had completed the sacrifices of burnt and peace offerings, he blessed the people in the name of GOD-of-the-Angel-Armies and handed out to each person in the crowd, men and women alike, a loaf of bread, a date cake, and a raisin cake. Then everyone went home.

David returned home to bless his family. Michal, Saul's daughter, came out to greet him: "How wonderfully the king has distinguished himself today—exposing himself to the eyes of the servants' maids like some burlesque street dancer!" David replied to Michal, "In GOD's presence I'll dance all I want! He chose me over your father and the rest of our family and made me prince over GOD's people, over Israel. Oh yes, I'll dance to GOD's glory—more recklessly even than this. And as far as I'm concerned . . . I'll gladly look like a fool . . . but among these maids you're so worried about, I'll be honored no end."

Michal, Saul's daughter, was barren the rest of her life.

think

- In Michal's place, would you have been embarrassed? Why or why not?
- What are some things you do—or don't do—to avoid embarrassment?
- Think of some times when you've been embarrassed. What role, if any, did "What will people think?" play in your feeling embarrassed?
- Is it ever appropriate to worry about what other people think? If so, when? If not, why not?

pray

Lord, I hate it when . . .

read approval addiction

From *The Life You've Always Wanted*, by John Ortberg[1]

Some people live in bondage to what others think of them.
The addiction takes many forms. If we find ourselves often getting hurt by what others say about us, by people expressing
other than glowing opinions about us, we probably have it. If
we habitually compare ourselves with other people, if we find
ourselves getting competitive in the most ordinary situations, we
probably have it. If we live with a nagging sense that we aren't
important enough or special enough, or we get envious of another's success, we probably have it. If we keep trying to impress
important people, we probably have it. If we are worried that
someone might think ill of us should he or she find out we are
an approval addict, we probably are. . . .

The alternative to this addiction—the life you've always
wanted—is the life of freedom. Lewis Smedes writes,

> One of the fine arts of gracious living is the art of liv-
> ing freely with our critics. When we have the grace to
> be free in the presence of those who judge our lives
> and evaluate our actions, we have Christian freedom.

think

- Which, if any, of the signs of approval addiction do you struggle with?
- What do you think makes some people addicted to approval?
  For instance, what might they be afraid of, or what might they
  believe about themselves?
- What's the difference between "living freely with our critics"
  and being too stubborn to listen to those who disagree with us?

think (continued)

pray

Lord, I really want to be . . .

read   pleasing the piety police

Galatians 2:11-16,19-21

*Both Paul (the writer of this passage) and Peter were Jews,
brought up to keep the kosher dietary laws, which at that
time included not even sharing a meal with non-Jews. Jewish
Christians in Antioch believed Christ had freed them from those
rules, but the more conservative believers in Jerusalem disagreed.*

Later, when Peter came to Antioch, I had a face-to-face confronta-
tion with him because he was clearly out of line. Here's the situation. Earlier, before certain persons had come from James, Peter
regularly ate with the non-Jews. But when that conservative group
came from Jerusalem, he cautiously pulled back and put as much
distance as he could manage between himself and his non-Jewish
friends. That's how fearful he was of the conservative Jewish clique
that's been pushing the old system of circumcision. Unfortunately,
the rest of the Jews in the Antioch church joined in that hypocrisy
so that even Barnabas was swept along in the charade.

But when I saw that they were not maintaining a steady,
straight course according to the Message, I spoke up to Peter in
front of them all: "If you, a Jew, live like a non-Jew when you're
not being observed by the watchdogs from Jerusalem, what right
do you have to require non-Jews to conform to Jewish customs just
to make a favorable impression on your old Jerusalem cronies?"

We Jews know that we have no advantage of birth over
"non-Jewish sinners." We know very well that we are not set
right with God by rule-keeping but only through personal faith
in Jesus Christ. How do we know? We tried it—and we had the
best system of rules the world has ever seen! Convinced that no
human being can please God by self-improvement, we believed
in Jesus as the Messiah so that we might be set right before God
by trusting in the Messiah, not by trying to be good. . . .

What actually took place is this: I tried keeping rules and working my head off to please God, and it didn't work. So I quit being

a "law man" so that I could be *God's* man. Christ's life showed me how, and enabled me to do it. I identified myself completely with him. Indeed, I have been crucified with Christ. My ego is no longer central. It is no longer important that I appear righteous before you or have your good opinion, and I am no longer driven to impress God. Christ lives in me. The life you see me living is not "mine," but it is lived by faith in the Son of God, who loved me and gave himself for me. I am not going to go back on that.

Is it not clear to you that to go back to that old rule-keeping, peer-pleasing religion would be an abandonment of everything personal and free in my relationship with God? I refuse to do that, to repudiate God's grace. If a living relationship with God could come by rule-keeping, then Christ died unnecessarily.

think

- Why do you think Peter changed his behavior when the conservatives came from Jerusalem?
- Suppose you believe that some activity is perfectly fine for Christians to do, and you do it with your friends. Then some other Christian friends of yours, who don't approve of that activity, come to visit. In a gathering with both groups of friends, would you do the activity or abstain? Why? (If your answer is, "It depends," describe what it depends on.)
- If "no human being can please God by self-improvement," why do people care about resisting temptation?
- What changes in Paul set him free from worrying about what people thought of him?

think (continued)

pray

Lord Jesus Christ, because you live in me . . .

read and the award for best actress goes to . . .

Matthew 6:1-6

"Be especially careful when you are trying to be good so that
you don't make a performance out of it. It might be good theater,
but the God who made you won't be applauding.

"When you do something for someone else, don't
call attention to yourself. You've seen them in action, I'm
sure—'playactors' I call them—treating prayer meeting and street
corner alike as a stage, acting compassionate as long as someone is watching, playing to the crowds. They get applause, true,
but that's all they get. When you help someone out, don't think
about how it looks. Just do it—quietly and unobtrusively. That is
the way your God, who conceived you in love, working behind
the scenes, helps you out.

"And when you come before God, don't turn that into a
theatrical production either. All these people making a regular
show out of their prayers, hoping for stardom! Do you think God
sits in a box seat?

"Here's what I want you to do: Find a quiet, secluded place
so you won't be tempted to role-play before God. Just be there
as simply and honestly as you can manage. The focus will shift
from you to God, and you will begin to sense his grace."

think

- What's wrong with wanting people to notice when you give
  money or help someone out?
- Is Jesus saying here that we should never pray aloud in pub-
  lic? Explain your view.
- Do you do anything in your church or small group to make
  others approve of what a good Christian you are? If so, what?
- What can small-group members do to make their group a safe
  place to get over the fear of what other people think?

think (continued)

pray

Father, just between you and me . . .

read   shhh, it's a secret

From *The Divine Conspiracy*, by Dallas Willard[2]

In both avoiding evil and doing good, our respect should be for God alone. We may think it is okay to avoid evil for fear of being seen, for in any case we do avoid the evil. But that only shows we have no respect for God and would disobey him but for the opinion of others. The basic principle is the same in both cases.

The discipline of secrecy will help us break the grip of human opinion over our souls and our actions. A discipline is an activity in our power that we do to enable us to do what we cannot do by direct effort. Jesus is here leading us into the discipline of secrecy. We from time to time practice doing things approved of in our religious circles—giving, praying, fasting, attending services of the church, and so on—but in such a way that no one knows. Thus our motivation and reward for doing these things cannot come from human beings. We are liberated from slavery to eyes, and then it does not matter whether people know or not. We learn to live constantly in this way.

think

- What do you think of the idea that "to avoid evil for fear of being seen" is morally worthless?
- What do you think of the idea that doing good because of peer pressure is also morally worthless?
- Dallas Willard says that we probably can't break the grip of human opinion by direct effort but that we can develop habits that will gradually do the job. How do you respond to the idea of addressing a temptation in this way?
- Does "the discipline of secrecy" seem like something that would be worthwhile for you to try? If not, why not? If so, how might you begin?

think (continued)

pray

Lord, I want to do things for the right reasons . . .

LIVE

what i want to discuss

What have you discovered this week that you definitely want to discuss with your small group? Write that here. Then begin your small-group discussion with these thoughts.

so what?

Use the following space to summarize the truths you uncovered about the grip of what other people think, how you feel about those truths, and where you need to begin in dealing with your situation. Review your "Beginning Place" if you need to remember where you began. How does God's truth affect the next step in your journey?

now what?

What is one practical thing you can do to respond to what you discovered? What concrete action can you take? Remember to think realistically—an admirable but unreachable goal is as good as no goal. Discuss your goal in your small group to further define it.

how?

How can your group—or even one other person—help you follow through with the goal you described? What support do you need? How will you measure the success of your plan? Write the details here.

doubting god's love

a reminder:

Before you dive into this study, spend a little time reviewing what you wrote in the previous lesson's "Live" section. How are you doing? Check with your small-group members and review your progress toward your goals. If necessary, adjust your goals and plans, and then recommit to them.

the beginning place

When we think of big temptations, doubting God's love may not seem to rank up there with greed and lust. But, in fact, it's the seeping acid that corrodes the foundation of our spiritual lives. Sometimes we'd rather watch television than pray because prayer feels like talking to a wall, because we don't think God cares what we feel or has any intention of responding, because he's way off there somewhere in heaven doing his own thing. Prayer doesn't seem like a treasured contact with the one who loves us passionately.

We worry about our jobs, our marriages, our children, and our future because we aren't convinced that a God with our best interests close to his heart is going to take care of us. We struggle with guilt and regret because we don't feel truly forgiven and we don't believe our past mistakes are being woven into a tapestry of beauty. Without a deep conviction that we're completely loved by a good God, it's tough to obey the top two commandments: "Love the Lord your God with all your passion and prayer and intelligence" and "Love others as well as you love yourself" (Matthew 22:37,39). It's hard to give away what we haven't received.

So take some time to reflect on your own awareness of God's love for you. How strongly are you convinced of that love? How do your actions reflect your confidence or your lack of it? What moves you to trust God's love or withhold full trust?

read   trust me

From *The God Who Loves You*, by Peter Kreeft[1]

When we believe God is something other than a lover, it is inevitable that we will sin. The devil tempted Eve to believe that God was selfish, arbitrary, and jealous in forbidding the forbidden fruit. Perhaps God was even evil, the devil implied, for he described God as "knowing good and evil" ([Genesis] 3:5). This probably means experiencing good and evil, as Adam "knew" Eve in Genesis 4:1, for example. Once Eve began to believe that God might not be pure love, an opening for sin was created. If all of me believes that God loves me, then nothing in me would want to disobey him. The way to conquer sin, therefore, is to build up faith in God's love.

think

- Why does doubting God's love make us vulnerable to other temptations?
- How does each of the following situations reflect a lack of confidence that God is fully loving and trustworthy?
  a. A woman overeats when she feels sad or overwhelmed.
  b. A single woman in her thirties decides to go ahead and sleep with her boyfriend.
  c. Having moved with her husband to a new town, a woman goes into debt decorating her new house so her new church friends will think she and her husband are successful.
  d. A woman avoids passionately longing for anything and busies herself with superb housekeeping, Bible study, a manicured lawn, and raising perfect children.
- Do you question God's love for you? If so, what moves you to question it?
- If you have a deep awareness of God's love for you, try to put into words how you got it.

think (continued)

pray

God, I want to believe . . .

read   god ruined me

Ruth 1:1-21

Once upon a time—it was back in the days when judges led
Israel—there was a famine in the land. A man from Bethlehem
in Judah left home to live in the country of Moab, he and his
wife and his two sons. The man's name was Elimelech; his wife's
name was Naomi; his sons were named Mahlon and Kilion—all
Ephrathites from Bethlehem in Judah. They all went to the country of Moab and settled there.

Elimelech died and Naomi was left, she and her two sons.
The sons took Moabite wives; the name of the first was Orpah,
the second Ruth. They lived there in Moab for the next ten years.
But then the two brothers, Mahlon and Kilion, died. Now the
woman was left without either her young men or her husband.

One day she got herself together, she and her two daughters-in-
law, to leave the country of Moab and set out for home; she had
heard that GOD had been pleased to visit his people and give
them food. And so she started out from the place she had been
living, she and her two daughters-in-law with her, on the road
back to the land of Judah.

After a short while on the road, Naomi told her two daughters-in-law, "Go back. Go home and live with your mothers. And
may GOD treat you as graciously as you treated your deceased
husbands and me. May GOD give each of you a new home and a
new husband!" She kissed them and they cried openly.

They said, "No, we're going on with you to your people."

But Naomi was firm: "Go back, my dear daughters. Why
would you come with me? Do you suppose I still have sons in
my womb who can become your future husbands? Go back, dear
daughters—on your way, please! I'm too old to get a husband.
Why, even if I said, 'There's still hope!' and this very night got a
man and had sons, can you imagine being satisfied to wait until
they were grown? Would you wait that long to get married again?

No, dear daughters; this is a bitter pill for me to swallow—more bitter for me than for you. GOD has dealt me a hard blow."

Again they cried openly. Orpah kissed her mother-in-law good-bye; but Ruth embraced her and held on.

Naomi said, "Look, your sister-in-law is going back home to live with her own people and gods; go with her."

But Ruth said, "Don't force me to leave you; don't make me go home. Where you go, I go; and where you live, I'll live. Your people are my people, your God is my god; where you die, I'll die, and that's where I'll be buried, so help me GOD—not even death itself is going to come between us!"

When Naomi saw that Ruth had her heart set on going with her, she gave in. And so the two of them traveled on together to Bethlehem.

When they arrived in Bethlehem the whole town was soon buzzing: "Is this really our Naomi? And after all this time!"

But she said, "Don't call me Naomi; call me Bitter. The Strong One has dealt me a bitter blow. I left here full of life, and GOD has brought me back with nothing but the clothes on my back. Why would you call me Naomi? God certainly doesn't. The Strong One ruined me."

think

- Do you think Naomi has good reasons to doubt God's love for her? Explain your thoughts.
- How does suffering like Naomi's affect a person's "I want what I want when I want it" attitude?
- What do you think Naomi should say to God in prayer?
- Do you have any experiences that make it hard for you to trust God's love? If so, what are they?

think (continued)

pray

Father, my suffering has . . .

read   i have a few questions

Job 30:20-28

> I shout for help, God, and get nothing, no answer!
>> I stand to face you in protest, and you give me a blank stare!
> You've turned into my tormenter—
>> you slap me around, knock me about.
> You raised me up so I was riding high
>> and then dropped me, and I crashed.
> I know you're determined to kill me,
>> to put me six feet under.
>
> What did I do to deserve this?
>> Did I ever hit anyone who was calling for help?
> Haven't I wept for those who live a hard life,
>> been heartsick over the lot of the poor?
> But where did it get me?
>> I expected good but evil showed up.
>> I looked for light but darkness fell.
> My stomach's in a constant churning, never settles down.
>> Each day confronts me with more suffering.
> I walk under a black cloud. The sun is gone.
>> I stand in the congregation and protest.

Habakkuk 1:2-4

> God, how long do I have to cry out for help
>> before you listen?
> How many times do I have to yell, "Help! Murder! Police!"
>> before you come to the rescue?
> Why do you force me to look at evil,
>> stare trouble in the face day after day?
> Anarchy and violence break out,
>> quarrels and fights all over the place.

Law and order fall to pieces.
    Justice is a joke.
The wicked have the righteous hamstrung
    and stand justice on its head.

think

- Why is Job upset? What about Habakkuk?
- What do you think about the way Job talks to God? What about the way Habakkuk does?
- Can you identify with anything Job or Habakkuk say? If so, what?
- Is it a sin to ask questions about God's love and goodness? What makes you say that?

pray

God, I'd like to know . . .

read you're unworthy — so what?

From *New Seeds of Contemplation*, by Thomas Merton[2]

In the true Christian vision of God's love, the idea of worthiness loses its significance. Revelation of the mercy of God makes the whole problem of worthiness something almost laughable: the discovery that worthiness is of no special consequence (since no one could ever, by himself, be strictly worthy to be loved with such a love) is a true liberation of the spirit. And until this discovery is made, until this liberation has been brought about by the divine mercy, man is imprisoned in hate.

"Love (III)," by George Herbert[3]

Love bade me welcome: yet my soul drew back,
    Guiltie of dust and sinne.
But quick-ey'd Love, observing me grow slack
    From my first entrance in,
Drew nearer to me, sweetly questioning,
    If I lack'd any thing.
A guest, I answer'd, worthy to be here:
    Love said, You shall be he.
I the unkinde, ungratefull? Ah my deare,
    I cannot look on thee.
Love took my hand, and smiling did reply,
    Who made the eyes but I?
Truth Lord, but I have marr'd them: let my shame
    Go where it doth deserve.
And know you not, sayes Love, who bore the blame?
    My dear, then I will serve.
You must sit down, sayes Love, and taste my meat:
    So I did sit and eat.

think

- For some of us, our doubts about God's love for us have less to do with suffering and more to do with our own unworthiness. Why does Thomas Merton think it's pointless to worry that you're unworthy of God's love?
- In the poem, how does Love address the author's concerns about his unworthiness?
- How do feelings of unworthiness affect a person's prayer life? How do they affect her ability to love others?
- Do feelings of unworthiness get in the way of your relationship with God? If so, how?

pray

Lord, my unworthiness . . .

read a crazy father

Luke 15:11-32

Then [Jesus] said, "There was once a man who had two sons. The younger said to his father, 'Father, I want right now what's coming to me.'

"So the father divided the property between them. It wasn't long before the younger son packed his bags and left for a distant country. There, undisciplined and dissipated, he wasted everything he had. After he had gone through all his money, there was a bad famine all through that country and he began to hurt. He signed on with a citizen there who assigned him to his fields to slop the pigs. He was so hungry he would have eaten the corncobs in the pig slop, but no one would give him any.

"That brought him to his senses. He said, 'All those farmhands working for my father sit down to three meals a day, and here I am starving to death. I'm going back to my father. I'll say to him, Father, I've sinned against God, I've sinned before you; I don't deserve to be called your son. Take me on as a hired hand.' He got right up and went home to his father.

"When he was still a long way off, his father saw him. His heart pounding, he ran out, embraced him, and kissed him. The son started his speech: 'Father, I've sinned against God, I've sinned before you; I don't deserve to be called your son ever again.'

"But the father wasn't listening. He was calling to the servants, 'Quick. Bring a clean set of clothes and dress him. Put the family ring on his finger and sandals on his feet. Then get a grain-fed heifer and roast it. We're going to feast! We're going to have a wonderful time! My son is here—given up for dead and now alive! Given up for lost and now found!' And they began to have a wonderful time.

"All this time his older son was out in the field. When the day's work was done he came in. As he approached the house, he heard the music and dancing. Calling over one of the houseboys, he asked what was going on. He told him, 'Your brother came home. Your father has ordered a feast—barbecued beef!—because he has him home safe and sound.'

"The older brother stalked off in an angry sulk and refused to join in. His father came out and tried to talk to him, but he wouldn't listen. The son said, 'Look how many years I've stayed here serving you, never giving you one moment of grief, but have you ever thrown a party for me and my friends? Then this son of yours who has thrown away your money on whores shows up and you go all out with a feast!'

"His father said, 'Son, you don't understand. You're with me all the time, and everything that is mine is yours—but this is a wonderful time, and we had to celebrate. This brother of yours was dead, and he's alive! He was lost, and he's found!'"

think

- How did the younger son underestimate his father's love for him?
- Why did the older son doubt his father's love for him?
- If you've been the kind of daughter who has wasted what your Father has given you, how easy is it for you to think of God celebrating your return? Why is that?
- If you've been the kind of daughter who has been good and never given your Father one moment of grief, how easy is it for you to believe him when he says, "You're with me all the time, and everything that is mine is yours"? Why is that?
- What do you think God wants to say to you?

pray

Father, your love . . .

read skull hill

Mark 15:22-39

The soldiers brought Jesus to Golgotha, meaning "Skull Hill."
They offered him a mild painkiller (wine mixed with myrrh), but
he wouldn't take it. And they nailed him to the cross. They divided up his clothes and threw dice to see who would get them.

They nailed him up at nine o'clock in the morning. The
charge against him—THE KING OF THE JEWS—was printed on a post-
er. Along with him, they crucified two criminals, one to his right,
the other to his left. People passing along the road jeered, shak-
ing their heads in mock lament: "You bragged that you could tear
down the Temple and then rebuild it in three days—so show us
your stuff! Save yourself! If you're really God's Son, come down
from that cross!"

The high priests, along with the religion scholars, were right
there mixing it up with the rest of them, having a great time
poking fun at him: "He saved others—but he can't save himself!
Messiah, is he? King of Israel? Then let him climb down from that
cross. We'll *all* become believers then!" Even the men crucified
alongside him joined in the mockery.

At noon the sky became extremely dark. The darkness lasted
three hours. At three o'clock, Jesus groaned out of the depths,
crying loudly, "*Eloi, Eloi, lama sabachthani?*" which means, "My
God, my God, why have you abandoned me?"

Some of the bystanders who heard him said, "Listen, he's
calling for Elijah." Someone ran off, soaked a sponge in sour
wine, put it on a stick, and gave it to him to drink, saying, "Let's
see if Elijah comes to take him down."

But Jesus, with a loud cry, gave his last breath. At that
moment the Temple curtain ripped right down the middle. When
the Roman captain standing guard in front of him saw that he
had quit breathing, he said, "This has to be the Son of God!"

think

- How, if at all, does this story affect you?
- Plenty of people read this story and don't sense God's love for them. Why not?
- What do you think moves a person from believing only theoretically that Christ died for her to being profoundly affected by this story?
- How can reflecting on the Cross change the way we view our suffering? How can it change the way we view our worthiness?

pray

Jesus, you went to the cross . . .

LIVE

what i want to discuss

What have you discovered this week that you definitely want to discuss with your small group? Write that here. Then begin your small-group discussion with these thoughts.

so what?

Use the following space to summarize the truths you uncovered about God's love, how you feel about those truths, and where you need to begin in dealing with your situation. Review your "Beginning Place" if you need to remember where you began. How does God's truth affect the next step in your journey?

now what?

What is one practical thing you can do to respond to what you discovered? What concrete action can you take? Remember to think realistically—an admirable but unreachable goal is as good as no goal. Discuss your goal in your small group to further define it.

how?

How can your group—or even one other person—help you follow through with the goal you described? What support do you need? How will you measure the success of your plan? Write the details here.

saying no

a reminder:

Before you dive into this study, spend a little time reviewing what you wrote in the previous lesson's "Live" section. How are you doing? Check with your small-group members and review your progress toward your goals. If necessary, adjust your goals and plans, and then recommit to them.

the beginning place

Okay, so we're inundated with temptations. We knew that already. How, in practical terms, do we steer around temptations minute by minute and live the free life God created us to live? Sometimes "Just Say No" is easy enough, but what about when it isn't?

If you look back through this study, you'll see a variety of strategies for resisting temptation:

- Examine the action in the light of Scripture to see if it is indeed a temptation to do wrong.
- Identify how the temptation is pushing your "I want what I want when I want it" buttons.
- Examine the temptation to see what false view of God it's promoting, especially the doubt it casts on God's love and goodness.
- Take your deepest hungers seriously rather than pretending they're not there, and go to God to get fed.

- Tell God honestly what you're feeling, and work the situation through with him.
- Identify what you long for sexually. If it's not currently available in a marriage, take your longings to God and accept no extramarital substitutes.
- Accept forgiveness for past sins, and practice gratitude for that forgiveness.
- If you have a deeply rooted habit that you can't uproot by direct willpower, cultivate practices that will eat away at those roots.
- Get support from your friends when you're tempted— especially when you feel sad, overwhelmed, lonely, or mad.
- Reflect on the Cross.

These are all great strategies, but ultimately they will fail if you lack one thing: the Holy Spirit. An unbeliever can study her temptations, honestly explore her longings and hurts, get support from her friends, and even use the Scriptures as a guide. Doing all that will take her a long way. But if she really wants the strength to say no to the temptations that most mess up her life, she needs to develop the habit of relying on the Holy Spirit.

Unfortunately, there is probably no aspect of this whole business that confuses Christians more than how to live by the Spirit. It sounds good—"Live by the Spirit"—but exactly how do you do it? Do you curl up on the couch with a good book and a cup of tea and wait for the Spirit to do his thing?

If only it were so. But the Bible shows us a curious dance between "I do it" and "The Spirit does it in and through me." So to begin this lesson, describe what comes to mind when you think of the Holy Spirit. Maybe you imagine wind in the trees, fire, an invisible force like electricity, or a blank screen. Maybe you feel you've experienced the Spirit, and maybe you don't. The subject might make you feel excited or frustrated. Whatever it is, describe your beginning place.

read   i choose

From *Perelandra*, by C. S. Lewis[1]

After the Lady of Perelandra chooses to obey Maleldil's command to live on floating islands rather than fixed land, both she and Dr. Ransom are able to reflect on why Maleldil allowed the temptation.

[Dr. Ransom] Certainly it must be part of the Divine plan that this happy creature should mature, should become more and more a creature of free choice, should become, in a sense, more distinct from God and from her husband in order thereby to be at one with them in a richer fashion. In fact, he had seen this very process going on from the moment at which he met her, and had, unconsciously, assisted it. This present temptation, if conquered, would itself be the next, and greatest, step in the same direction: an obedience freer, more reasoned, more conscious than any she had known before, was being put in her power. . . .

[The Lady] "The reason for not yet living on the Fixed Land is now so plain. How could I wish to live there except because it was Fixed? And why should I desire the Fixed except to make sure—to be able on one day to command where I should be the next and what should happen to me? It was to reject the waves—to draw my hand out of Maleldil's, to say to Him, 'not thus, but thus'—to put in our own power what times should roll towards us. . . . That would have been cold love and feeble trust. And how could we ever have climbed back into love and trust again?"

think

- Why did Maleldil (God) allow the Lady to be genuinely tempted to disobey him?
- Why might a person prefer to live on fixed land rather than on islands floating in a vast sea? In what ways, if any, do you identify with this desire?

- What is the role of free choice in resisting temptation?
- What's the difference between being carried in God's will and walking with it?

pray

God, I choose . . .

read   playing by the rules

Galatians 3:2-5,9-12

Let me put this question to you: How did your new life begin?
Was it by working your heads off to please God? Or was it by
responding to God's Message to you? Are you going to continue
this craziness? For only crazy people would think they could
complete by their own efforts what was begun by God. If you
weren't smart enough or strong enough to begin it, how do you
suppose you could perfect it? Did you go through this whole
painful learning process for nothing? It is not yet a total loss, but
it certainly will be if you keep this up!

Answer this question: Does the God who lavishly provides
you with his own presence, his Holy Spirit, working things in
your lives you could never do for yourselves, does he do these
things because of your strenuous moral striving *or* because you
trust him to do them in you? . . .

So those now who live by faith are blessed along with
Abraham, who lived by faith—this is no new doctrine! And that
means that anyone who tries to live by his own effort, indepen-
dent of God, is doomed to failure. . . .

The obvious impossibility of carrying out such a moral program should make it plain that no one can sustain a relationship
with God that way. The person who lives in right relationship
with God does it by embracing what God arranges for him.
Doing things for God is the opposite of entering into what God
does for you. Habakkuk had it right: "The person who believes
God, is set right by God—and that's the real life." Rule-keeping
does not naturally evolve into living by faith, but only perpetu-
ates itself in more and more rule-keeping, a fact observed in
Scripture: "The one who does these things [rule-keeping] contin-
ues to live by them."

think

- Why is trust in God essential in order for the Spirit to be active in us?
- How does what Paul says here about trust or faith compare to what the Lady of Perelandra (see previous "Read" section) said about trust?
- Despite the availability of the Holy Spirit, why might a person prefer to work her head off keeping rules?
- Was the Lady of Perelandra working at rule keeping in the way Paul condemns? Explain your view.

pray

Father, I want to trust you . . .

read   free spirit

Galatians 5:13-18

It is absolutely clear that God has called you to a free life. Just make sure that you don't use this freedom as an excuse to do whatever you want to do and destroy your freedom. Rather, use your freedom to serve one another in love; that's how freedom grows. For everything we know about God's Word is summed up in a single sentence: Love others as you love yourself. That's an act of true freedom. If you bite and ravage each other, watch out—in no time at all you will be annihilating each other, and where will your precious freedom be then?

My counsel is this: Live freely, animated and motivated by God's Spirit. Then you won't feed the compulsions of selfishness. For there is a root of sinful self-interest in us that is at odds with a free spirit, just as the free spirit is incompatible with selfishness. These two ways of life are antithetical, so that you cannot live at times one way and at times another way according to how you feel on any given day. Why don't you choose to be led by the Spirit and so escape the erratic compulsions of a law-dominated existence?

think

- How does Paul define freedom? How does that compare with other definitions you've heard?
- Does Paul agree or disagree with what Perelandra says about free choice? What makes you say that?
- Selfishness is treating our self and our survival as the center of our universe, our most important concern. Why does selfishness keep a person from accessing the Holy Spirit's help?
- Why is selfishness so hard to shake off?

think (continued)

pray

Spirit of God, the freedom I want . . .

read   humility

From *Lifestyle Discipleship*, by Jim Petersen[2]

Does it surprise you that humility is the response God is watching for? How about repentance, or confession? Humility precedes them both. Neither can happen without humility.

Humility is the one response I am still capable of making even when I'm at my worst, even while I'm in the midst of struggle. It is an admission of my weakness and dependence. The Holy Spirit responds to this admission. He comes in and empowers me to respond to the current struggle in His favor.

There can be no deliverance without humility. It takes humility to be honest and come clean. How difficult it is to say, "I was wrong!" But these words take us out of our darkness and into the light. They bring us out into the open before God and our sisters and brothers. Humility sets the stage for the Holy Spirit's direction and empowerment. Once our old natures have been subdued, reason and truth can have a voice. As we humble ourselves, God can quit resisting us and begin to hear us instead.

think

- What is humility? How is it different from self-hatred or being a helpless doormat?
- How do you respond to the idea that the Holy Spirit can't or won't help us if we don't have humility?
- What past experiences might make a woman prefer self-reliance to humility?
- In lesson 8, we've looked at three things that can hinder us from accessing the Spirit's help: lack of trust, selfishness, and lack of humility. Which of these do you most need to address?

think (continued)

pray
Holy Spirit, humbling myself . . .

read   how can we lose?

Romans 8:26-32

Meanwhile, the moment we get tired in the waiting, God's Spirit is right alongside helping us along. If we don't know how or what to pray, it doesn't matter. He does our praying in and for us, making prayer out of our wordless sighs, our aching groans. He knows us far better than we know ourselves, knows our pregnant condition, and keeps us present before God. That's why we can be so sure that every detail in our lives of love for God is worked into something good.

God knew what he was doing from the very beginning. He decided from the outset to shape the lives of those who love him along the same lines as the life of his Son. The Son stands first in the line of humanity he restored. We see the original and intended shape of our lives there in him. After God made that decision of what his children should be like, he followed it up by calling people by name. After he called them by name, he set them on a solid basis with himself. And then, after getting them established, he stayed with them to the end, gloriously completing what he had begun.

So, what do you think? With God on our side like this, how can we lose? If God didn't hesitate to put everything on the line for us, embracing our condition and exposing himself to the worst by sending his own Son, is there anything else he wouldn't gladly and freely do for us?

think

- Why is the Holy Spirit's help with prayer so valuable?
- Does saying no to sin ultimately make you more fully yourself, or less? Why?
- Is there anything in this passage that helps you develop trust, humility, or unselfishness? If so, what?

think (continued)

pray

Lord, I need . . .

LIVE

This is the end of *Peeking into a Box of Chocolates*, but it's not the end of the story for you. Hopefully, you've discovered some truths about your life and seen opportunities for positive change. If you're like most people, though, sticking to the status quo is far more comfortable than changing. What you've gained from this study will soon be left in the dust unless you really want your life to be different.

• What thoughts about the Holy Spirit do you definitely want to discuss with your small group?

• You probably can't give equal attention to all of the issues raised in this study. What are the key things God has been trying to say to you about one or more of the following?

Self-centeredness

Consumerism

Food

Giving up

Sex

What people think of you

Trusting God's love

Humility

Temptation as a whole

• How have your practical steps in these areas been going?

• How will God's truth influence what you do in the next week, next month, and next year?

• How can your small group help you get there?

notes

lesson 1

1. C. S. Lewis, *Perelandra* (New York: Macmillan, 1944), p. 112.
2. Dallas Willard, *Renovation of the Heart: Putting on the Character of Christ* (Colorado Springs, Colo.: NavPress, 2002), pp. 51-52, 56.

lesson 2

1. Linda Kulman, "Our Consuming Interest," *U.S. News and World Report*, June 28/July 5, 2004, pp. 59-60.
2. Victoria Clayton, "Psychology by the Square Foot," *Los Angeles Times*, August 10, 2003, p. 12.
3. Andy Crouch, "Consuming Passions," *Christianity Today*, July 9, 2001, p. 49.

lesson 3

1. Michael Pollan, "Our National Eating Disorder," *The New York Times*, October 17, 2004.
2. Cathy Newman, "Why Are We So Fat?" *National Geographic*, August 2004, pp. 48-61.
3. Karen Lee-Thorp and Cynthia Hicks, *Why Beauty Matters* (Colorado Springs, Colo.: NavPress, 1997), pp. 139-140.
4. Anne Lamott, *Traveling Mercies: Some Thoughts on Faith* (New York: Anchor Books, 1999), pp. 190-194.

lesson 4

1. Vinita Hampton Wright, *Grace at Bender Springs: A Novel* (Nashville: Broadman, Holman, 1999), pp. 145-146.
2. Brent Curtis and John Eldredge, *The Sacred Romance: Drawing Closer to the Heart of God* (Nashville: Nelson, 1997), pp. 126, 130.
3. Garret Keizer, "The Enigma of Anger," *Books and Culture*, September/October 2002, p. 9.

lesson 5
1. Shirley P. Glass, Ph.D., with Jean Coppock Staeheli, *NOT "Just Friends": Rebuilding Trust and Recovering Your Sanity After Infidelity* (New York: The Free Press, 2003), pp. 23-24, 31.
2. Paula Rinehart, *Sex and the Soul of a Woman: The Reality of Love and Romance in an Age of Casual Sex* (Grand Rapids, Mich.: Zondervan, 2004), pp. 29-30.
3. Lauren F. Winner, "Solitary Refinement," *Christianity Today*, June 11, 2001, p. 34.

lesson 6
1. John Ortberg, *The Life You've Always Wanted* (Grand Rapids, Mich.: Zondervan, 1997), p. 152.
2. Dallas Willard, *The Divine Conspiracy: Rediscovering Our Hidden Life in God* (San Francisco: HarperSanFrancisco, 1998), p. 200.

lesson 7
1. Peter Kreeft, *The God Who Loves You: Love Divine, All Loves Excelling* (Ann Arbor, Mich.: Servant, 1988), p. 139.
2. Thomas Merton, excerpt from *New Seeds of Contemplation*, in *A Thomas Merton Reader*, ed. Thomas P. McDonnell (Garden City, N.Y.: Image, 1974), p. 322.
3. George Herbert, "Love (III)," *Poems of George Herbert* (London: Oxford University Press, 1961), p. 180.

lesson 8
1. C. S. Lewis, *Perelandra* (New York: Macmillan, 1944), pp. 133, 208-209.
2. Jim Petersen, *Lifestyle Discipleship: The Challenges of Following Jesus in Today's World* (Colorado Springs, Colo.: NavPress, 1993), pp. 111-112.

Another life-shaping title in the
REAL LIFE STUFF FOR WOMEN *series:*
Coming to God's terms with the realities
that shape women's lives today.

Running Nowhere in Every Direction
On Stress
1-57683-836-6

We seem to be running as fast as we can — to work, school, church, sports, music lessons, and the mall. But the faster we run, the more many of us realize we're really running nowhere.

This refreshing new discussion guide encourages us to join with other women to discover God's ways to get off the treadmill. Bringing together literary and cultural insights, conversation starters, and key passages from *The Message*, this book will help you discover what God has to say about the stress in your life and about running nowhere and walking somewhere with God.

Visit your local Christian bookstore,
call NavPress at 1-800-366-7788,
or log on to www.navpress.com to purchase.

To locate a Christian bookstore near you, call 1-800-991-7747.

NAVPRESS ®
BRINGING TRUTH TO LIFE
w w w . n a v p r e s s . c o m